INTRODUCTION

Since the pages of this book was digitized from a very old original, the pages here may look a little funny at times. Rest assured we did our best to format the original book into modern form as best allowed by the current processes available.

Although each page of this book was digitized from the original edition this reprint is in no way endorsed by or associated with the original author Clarence B. Edwords.

Ross Brown

Introduction and Cover Art Copyright 2008 -
All rights reserved.
TheDesignHouse
ISBN 1440472629

For regular updates on new reprint editions of
vintage cookbooks,
vintage cocktail books,
vintage bar books
vintage wine books and
vintage drinks books
please visit

www.VintageCocktailBooks.com

THE OLD
COBWEB PALACE AT
MEIGGS'S WHARF

BOHEMIAN SAN FRANCISCO

ITS RESTAURANTS AND THEIR MOST FAMOUS RECIPES • THE ELEGANT ART OF DINING

By
CLARENCE E. EDWORDS

PAUL ELDER AND COMPANY
PUBLISHERS • SAN FRANCISCO

COPYRIGHT, 1914, BY
PAUL ELDER AND COMPANY
SAN FRANCISCO

DEDICATION
TO WHOM SHALL I DEDICATE THIS BOOK?
TO SOME GOOD FRIEND? TO SOME PLEASANT COMPANION?
TO NONE OF THESE, FOR FROM THEM CAME NOT THE INSPIRATION.
TO WHOM, THEN?
TO THE BEST OF ALL BOHEMIAN COMRADES,
MY WIFE.

FOREWORD

No apologies are offered for this book. In fact, we rather like it. Many years have been spent in gathering this information, and naught is written in malice, nor through favoritism, our expressions of opinion being unbiased by favor or compensation. We have made our own investigation and given our own ideas.

That our opinion does not coincide with that of others does not concern us in the least, for we are pleased only with that which pleases us, and not that with which others say we ought to be pleased.

If this sound egotistical we are sorry, for it is not meant in that way. We believe that each and every individual should judge for him or herself, considering ourselves fortunate that our ideas and tastes are held in common.

San Franciscans, both residential and transient, are a pleasure-loving people, and dining out is a distinctive feature of their pleasure. With hundreds of restaurants to select from, each specializing on some particular dish, or some peculiar mode of preparation, one often becomes bewildered and turns to familiar names on the menu card rather than venture into fields that are new, of strange and rare dishes whose unpronounceable names of themselves frequently are sufficient to discourage those unaccustomed to the art and science of cooking practiced by those whose lives have been spent devising means of tickling fastidious palates of a city of gourmets.

In order that those who come within our gates, and many others who have resided here in blindness for years, may know where to go and what to eat, and that they may carry away with them a knowledge of how to prepare some of the dishes pleasing to the taste and nourishing to the body, that have spread San Francisco's fame over the world, we have decided to set down the result of our experience and study of

FOREWORD

our Bohemian population and their ways, and also tell where to find and how to order the best special dishes.

Over North Beach way we asked the chef of a little restaurant how he cooked crab. He replied:

"The right way."

One often wonders how certain dishes are cooked and we shall tell you "the right way."

It is hoped that when you read what is herein written some of our pleasure may be imparted to you, and with this hope the story of San Francisco's Bohemianism is presented.

CLARENCE E. EDWORDS.
*San Francisco, California,
September 22, 1914.*

Our Toast

*Not to the Future, nor to the Past;
No drink of Joy or Sorrow;
We drink alone to what will last;
Memories on the Morrow.
Let us live as Old Time passes;
To the Present let Bohemia bow.
Let us raise on high our glasses
To Eternity—the ever-living Now.*

CONTENTS

FOREWORD	IX
THE GOOD GRAY CITY	3
THE LAND OF BOHEMIA	6
AS IT WAS IN THE BEGINNING	8
WHEN THE GRINGO CAME	10
EARLY ITALIAN IMPRESSION	12
BIRTH OF THE FRENCH RESTAURANT	16
AT THE CLIFF HOUSE	21
SOME ITALIAN RESTAURANTS	23
IMPRESS OF MEXICO	29
ON THE BARBARY COAST	33
THE CITY THAT WAS PASSES	35
SANG THE SWAN SONG	36
BOHEMIA OF THE PRESENT	41
AS IT IS IN GERMANY	46
IN THE HEART OF ITALY	50
A BREATH OF THE ORIENT	54
ARTISTIC JAPAN	57
OLD AND NEW PALACE	60
AT THE HOTEL ST. FRANCIS	63
AMID THE BRIGHT LIGHTS	65
AROUND LITTLE ITALY	66
WHERE FISH COME IN	76
FISH IN THEIR VARIETY	80
LOBSTERS AND LOBSTERS	85
KING OF SHELL FISH	87
LOBSTER IN MINIATURE	89
CLAMS AND ABALONES	91
WHERE FISH ABOUND	94
SOME FOOD VARIANTS	97

CONTENTS

ABOUT DINING	100
SOMETHING ABOUT COOKING	106
TOLD IN A WHISPER	110
OUT OF NOTHING	115
PASTE MAKES WAIST	117
TIPS AND TIPPING	119
THE MYTHICAL LAND	121
APPENDIX (HOW TO SERVE WINES, RECIPES) . .	125
INDEX	137

BOHEMIAN SAN FRANCISCO

*"The best of all ways
To lengthen our days
Is to steal a few hours
From the night, my dear."*

SAN FRANCISCO

San Francisco! Is there a land where the magic of that name has not been felt? Bohemian San Francisco! Pleasure-loving San Francisco! Care-free San Francisco! Yet withal the city where liberty never means license and where Bohemianism is not synonymous with Boorishness.

THE GOOD GRAY CITY

It was in Paris that a world traveler said to us:

"San Francisco! That wonderful city where you get the best there is to eat, served in a manner that enhances its flavor and establishes it forever in your memory."

Were one to write of San Francisco and omit mention of its gustatory delights the whole world would protest, for in San Francisco eating is an art and cooking a science, and he who knows not what San Francisco provides knows neither art nor science.

Here have congregated the world's greatest chefs, and when one exclaims in ecstacy over a wonderful flavor found in some dingy restaurant, let him not be surprised if he learn that the chef who concocted the dish boasts royal decoration for tickling the palate of some epicurean ruler of foreign land.

And why should San Francisco have achieved this distinction in the minds of the gourmets?

Do not other cities have equally as good chefs, and do not the people of other cities have equally as fine gastronomic taste?

They have all this but with them is lacking "atmosphere."

Where do we find such romanticism as in San Francisco? Where do we find so many strange characters and happenings? All lending almost mystic charm to the environment surrounding queer little restaurants, where rare dishes are served, and where one feels that he is in foreign land, even though he be in the center of a high representative American city.

BOHEMIAN

San Francisco's cosmopolitanism is peculiar to itself. Here are represented the nations of earth in such distinctive colonies that one might well imagine himself possessed of the magic carpet told of in Arabian Nights Tales, as he is transported in the twinkling of an eye from country to country. It is but a step across a street from America into Japan, then another step into China. Cross another street and you are in Mexico, close neighbor to France. Around the corner lies Italy, and from Italy you pass to Lombardy, and on to Greece. So it goes until one feels that he has been around the world in an afternoon.

THE GOOD
GRAY
CITY

But the stepping across the street and one passes from one land to the other, finding all the peculiar characteristics of the various countries as indelibly fixed as if they were thousands of miles away. Speech, manners, customs, costumes and religions change with startling rapidity, and as you enter into the life of the nation you find that each has brought the best of its gastronomy for your delectation.

San Francisco has called to the world for its best, and the response has been so prompt that no country has failed to send its tribute and give the best thought of those who cater to the men and women who know.

This aggregation of cuisinaire, gathered where is to be found a most wonderful variety of food products in highest state of excellence, has made San Francisco the Mecca for lovers of gustatory delights, and this is why the name of San Francisco is known wherever men and women sit at table.

It has taken us years of patient research to learn how these chefs prepare their combinations of fish, flesh, fowl, and herbs, in order that we might put them down, giving recipes of dishes whose memories linger in the minds of world wanderers, and to which their

SAN FRANCISCO

thoughts revert with a sigh as they partake of unsatisfactory viands in other countries and other cosmopolitan cities.

THE GOOD GRAY CITY

Those to whom only the surface of things is visible are prone to express wonder at the love and enthusiasm of the San Franciscan for his home city. The casual visitor cannot understand the enchantment, the mystery, the witchery that holds one; they do not know that we steal the hours from the night to lengthen our days because the gray, whispering wraiths of fog hold for us the very breath of life; they do not know that the call of the wind, and of the sea, and of the air, is the inspiration that makes San Francisco the pleasure-ground of the world.

It is this that makes San Francisco the home of Bohemia, and whether it be in the early morning hours as one rises to greet the first gray streaks of dawn, or as the sun drops through the Golden Gate to its ocean bed, so slowly that it seems loth to leave; whether it be in the broad glare of noon-day sun, or under the dazzling blaze of midnight lights, San Francisco ever holds out her arms, wide in welcome, to those who see more in life than the dull routine of working each day in order that they may gain sufficient to enable them to work again on the morrow.

BOHEMIAN

Bohemia! What vulgarities are perpetrated in thy name! How abused is the word! Because of a misconception of an idea it has suffered more than any other in the English language. It has done duty in describing almost every form of license and licentiousness. It has been the cloak of debauchery and the excuse for sex degradation. It has been so misused as to bring the very word into disrepute.

THE LAND OF BOHEMIA

To us Bohemianism means the naturalism of refined people.

That it may be protected from vulgarians Society prescribes conventional rules and regulations, which, like morals, change with environment.

Bohemianism is the protest of naturalism against the too rigid, and, oft-times, absurd restrictions established by Society.

The Bohemian requires no prescribed rules, for his or her innate gentility prevents those things Society guards against. In Bohemia men and women mingle in good fellowship and camaraderie without finding the sex question a necessary topic of conversation. They do not find it necessary to push exhilaration to intoxication; to increase their animation to boisterousness. Their lack of conventionality does not tend to boorishness.

Some of the most enjoyable Bohemian affairs we know of have been full dress gatherings, carefully planned and delightfully carried out; others have been impromptu, neither the hour, the place, nor the dress being taken into consideration.

The unrefined get everywhere, even into the drawing rooms of royalty, consequently we must expect to meet them in Bohemia. But the true Bohemian has a way of forgetting to meet obnoxious personages and, as a rule, is more choice in the selection of associates

SAN FRANCISCO

than the vaunted "400." With the Bohemian but one thing counts: Fitness. Money, position, personal appearance and even brains are of no avail if there be the bar sinister—unfit.

THE LAND OF BOHEMIA

In a restaurant, one evening, a number of men and women were seated conspicuously at a table in the center of the room. Flowing neckties such as are affected by Parisian art students were worn by the men; all were coarse, loud and much in evidence. They not only attracted attention by their loudness and outre actions, but they called notice by pelting other diners with missiles of bread. To us they were the last word in vulgarity, but to a young woman who had come to the place because she had heard it was "so Bohemian" they were ideal, and she remarked to her companion:

"I do so love to associate with real Bohemians like these. Can't we get acquainted with them?"

"Sure," was the response. "All we have to do is to buy them a drink."

In San Francisco there are Bohemians and Near-Bohemians, and if you are like the young woman mentioned you are apt to miss the real and take the imitation for the genuine article.

We mean no derogation of San Francisco's restaurants when we say that San Francisco's highest form of Bohemianism is rarely in evidence in restaurants. We have enjoyed wonderful Bohemian dinners in restaurants, but the other diners were not aware of it. Some far more interesting gatherings have been in the rooms of Bohemian friends. Not always is it the artistic combination of famous chef that brings greatest delight, for we have as frequently had pleasure over a supper of some simple dish in the attic room of a good friend.

This brings us to the crux of Bohemianism. It depends so little on environment that it means nothing, and so much on companionship that it means all.

BOHEMIAN

To achieve a comprehensive idea of San Francisco's Bohemianism let us divide its history into five eras.

AS IT WAS
IN THE
BEGINNING

First we have the old Spanish days—the days "before the Gringo came." Then reigned conviviality held within most discreet bounds of convention, and it would be a misnomer, indeed, to call the pre-pioneer days of San Francisco "Bohemian" in any sense of the word.

Courtesy unfailing, good-fellowship always in tune, and lavish hospitality, marked the days of the Dons—those wonderfully considerate hosts who always placed a pile of gold and silver coins on the table of the guest chamber, in order that none might go away in need. Their feasts were events of careful consideration and long preparation, and those whose memories carry them back to the early days, recall bounteous loading of tables when festal occasion called for display.

Lips linger lovingly over such names as the Vallejos, the Picos, and those other Spanish families who spread their hospitality with such wondrous prodigality that their open welcome became a by-word in all parts of the West.

But it was not in the grand fiestas that the finest and most palatable dishes were to be found. In the family of each of these Spanish Grandees were culinary secrets known to none except the "Senora de la Casa," and transmitted by her to her sons and daughters.

We have considered ourselves fortunate in being taken into the confidence of one of the descendants of Senora Benicia Vallejo, and honored with some of her prize recipes, which find place in this book, not as the famous recipe of some Bohemian restaurants but as the tribute to the spirit of the land that made those Bohemian restaurants possible. Of these there is no more tasty and satisfying dish than Spanish Eggs, prepared as follows:

SAN FRANCISCO

Empty a can of tomatoes in a frying pan; thicken with bread and add two or three small green peppers and an onion sliced fine. Add a little butter and salt to taste. Let this simmer gently and then carefully break on top the number of eggs desired. Dip the simmering tomato mixture over the eggs until they are cooked.

SPANISH EGGS

Another favorite recipe of Mrs. Vallejo was Spanish Beefsteak prepared as follows:

Cut the steak into pieces the size desired for serving. Place these pieces on a meat board and sprinkle liberally with flour. With a wooden corrugated mallet beat the flour into the steak. Fry the steak in a pan with olive oil. In another frying pan, at the same time, fry three good-sized onions and three green peppers. When the steak is cooked sufficiently put it to one side of the pan and let the oil run to the other side. On the oil pour sufficient water to cover the meat and add the onions and peppers, letting all simmer for a few minutes. Serve on hot platter.

SPANISH BEEFSTEAK

Spanish mode of cooking rice is savory and most palatable, and Mrs. Vallejo's recipe for this is as follows:

Slice together three good-sized onions and three small green peppers. Fry them in olive oil. Take one-half cup of rice and boil it until nearly done, then drain it well and add it to the frying onions and peppers. Fry all together until thoroughly brown, which will take some time. Season with salt and serve.

SPANISH RICE

These three recipes are given because they are simple and easily prepared. Many complex recipes could be given, and some of these will appear in the part of the book devoted to recipes, but when one considers the simplicity of the recipes mentioned, it can readily be seen that it takes little preparation to get something out of the ordinary.

9

BOHEMIAN

To its pioneer days much of San Francisco's Bohemian spirit is due. When the cry of "Gold" rang around the world adventurous wanderers of all lands answered the call, and during the year following Marshall's discovery two thousand ships sailed into San Francisco Bay, many to be abandoned on the beach by the gold-mad throng, and it was in some of these deserted sailing vessels that San Francisco's restaurant life had its inception. With the immediately succeeding years the horde of gold hunters was augmented by those who brought necessities and luxuries to exchange for the yellow metal given up by the streams flowing from the Mother Lode. With them also came cooks to prepare delectable dishes for those who had passed the flap-jack stage, and desired the good things of life to repay them for the hardships, privations and dearth of woman's companionship. As the male human was largely dominant in numbers it was but natural that they should gather together for companionship, and here began the Bohemian spirit that has marked the city for its own to the present day.

WHEN THE GRINGO CAME

These men were all individualists, and their individualism has been transmitted to their offspring together with independence of action. Hence comes the Bohemianism born of individuality and independence.

It was only natural that the early San Franciscans should foregather where good cheer was to be found, and the old El Dorado House, at Portsmouth Square, was really what may be called the first Bohemian restaurant of the city. So well was this place patronized and so exorbitant the prices charged that twenty-five thousand dollars a month was not considered an impossible rental.

Next in importance was the most fashionable restaurant of early days, the Iron House. It was built of heavy sheet iron that had been brought around the

SAN FRANCISCO

Horn in a sailing vessel, and catered well, becoming for several years the most famed restaurant of the city. Here, in Montgomery street, between Jackson and Pacific, was the rendezvous of pioneers, and here the Society of California Pioneers had its inception, receiving impressions felt to the present day in San Francisco and California history. Here, also, was first served Chicken in the Shell, the dish from which so many later restaurants gained fame. The recipe for this as prepared by the Iron House is still extant, and we are indebted to a lady, who was a little girl when that restaurant was waning, whose mother secured the recipe. It was prepared as follows:

WHEN THE GRINGO CAME

Into a kettle containing a quart of water put a young chicken, one sliced onion, a bay leaf, two cloves, a blade of mace and six pepper-corns. Simmer in the covered kettle for one hour and set aside to cool. When cool remove the meat from the bones, rejecting the skin. Cut the meat into small dice. Mix in a saucepan, over a fire without browning, a tablespoonful of butter, a tablespoonful of flour, then add half a pint of cream. Stir this constantly until it boils, then add a truffle, two dozen mushrooms chopped fine, a dash of white pepper and then the dice of chicken. Let the whole stand in a bain marie, or chafing dish, until quite hot. Add the yolks of two eggs and let cook two minutes. Stir in half a glass of sherry and serve in cockle shells.

CHICKEN IN THE SHELL

BOHEMIAN

EARLY ITALIAN IMPRESSION

Almost coincident with the opening of the Iron House an Italian named Bazzuro took possession of one of the stranded sailing vessels encumbering the Bay, and anchored it out in the water at the point where Davis and Pacific streets now intersect. He opened a restaurant which immediately attracted attention and gained good reputation for its service and its cooking. Later, when the land was filled in, Bazzuro built a house at almost the same spot and opened his restaurant there, continuing it up to the time of the great fire in 1906.

After the fire one of the earliest restaurants to be established in that part of the city was Bazzuro's, at the same corner, and it is still run by the family, who took charge after the death of the original proprietor. Here one can get the finest Italian peasant meal in the city, and many of the Italian merchants and bankers still go there for their luncheons every day, preferring it to the more pretentious establishments.

The French peasant style came a little later, beginning in a little dining room opened in Washington street, just above Kearny, by a French woman whose name was a carefully guarded secret. She was known far and wide as "Ma Tanta" (My Aunt). Her cooking was considered the best of all in the city, and her patrons sat at a long common table, neat and clean to the last degree. Peasant style of serving was followed. First appeared Ma Tanta with a great bowl of salad which she passed around, each patron helping himself. This was followed by an immense tureen of soup, held aloft in the hands of Ma Tanta, and again each was his own waiter. Fish, entree, roast, and dessert, were served in the same manner, and with the black coffee Ma Tanta changed from servitor to hostess and sat with her guests and discussed the topics of the day on equal terms.

SAN FRANCISCO

In California street, just below Dupont, the California House boasted a great chef in the person of John Somali, who in later years opened the Maison Riche, a famous restaurant that went out of existence in the fire of 1906. Gourmets soon discovered that the California House offered something unusual and it became a famed resort. Somali's specialties were roast turkey, chateaubriand steak and coffee frappe. It is said of his turkeys that their flavor was of such excellence that one of the gourmands of that day, Michael Reece, would always order two when he gave a dinner—one for his guests and one for himself. It is also said that our well-beloved Bohemian, Rafael Weill, still holds memories of the old California House, of which he was an habitue, and from whose excellent chef he learned to appreciate the art and science of cooking as evidenced by the breakfasts and dinners with which he regales his guests at the present day.

EARLY ITALIAN IMPRESSION

But many of the hardy pioneers were of English and American stock and preferred the plainer foods of their old homes to the highly seasoned dishes of the Latin chefs, and to cater to this growing demand the Nevada was opened in Pine street between Montgomery and Kearny. This place became noted for its roast beef and also for its corned beef and cabbage, which was said to be of most excellent flavor.

Most famous of all the old oyster houses was Mannings, at the corner of Pine and Webb streets. He specialized in oysters and many of his dishes have survived to the present day. It is said that the style now called "Oysters Kirkpatrick," is but a variant of Manning's "Oyster Salt Roast."

At the corner of California and Sansome streets, where now stands the Bank of California, was the Tehama House, one of the most famous of the city's

BOHEMIAN

early hostelries, whose restaurant was famed for its excellence. The Tehama House was the rendezvous of army and navy officers and high state officials. Lieutenant John Derby, of the United States Army, one of the most widely known western authors of that day, made it his headquarters. Derby wrote under the names of "John Phoenix," and "Squibob."

EARLY ITALIAN IMPRESSION

Perini's, in Post street between Grant avenue and Stockton, specialized in pastes and veal rissotto, and was much patronized by uptown men.

The original Marchand began business in a little room in Dupont street, between Jackson and Washington, which district at that time had not been given over to the Chinese, and he cooked over a charcoal brazier, in his window, in view of passing people who were attracted by the novelty and retained by the good cooking. With the extension of his fame he found his room too small and he rented a cottage at Bush and Dupont street, but his business grew so rapidly that he was compelled to move to more commodious quarters at Post and Dupont and later to a much larger place at Geary and Stockton, where he enjoyed good patronage until the fire destroyed his place. There is now a restaurant in Geary street near Mason which has on its windows in very small letters "Michael, formerly of," and then in bold lettering, "Marchands." But Michael has neither the art nor the viands that made Marchands famous, and he is content to say that his most famous dish is tripe—just plain, plebeian tripe.

Christian Good, at Washington and Kearny, Big John, at Merchant street between Montgomery and Sansome, Marshall's Chop House, in the old Center Market, and Johnson's Oyster House, in a basement at Clay and Leidesdorff streets, were all noted places and much patronized, the latter laying the foundation of one of San

SAN FRANCISCO

Francisco's "First Families." Martin's was much patronized by the Old Comstock crowd, and this was the favorite dining place of the late William C. Ralston.

EARLY ITALIAN IMPRESSION

One of the most famous restaurants of the early '70s was the Mint, in Commercial street, between Montgomery and Kearny, where the present restaurant of the same name is located. It was noted for its Southern cooking and was the favorite resort of W. W. Foote and other prominent Southerners. The kitchen was presided over by old Billy Jackson, an old-time Southern darkey, who made a specialty of fried chicken, cream gravy, and corn fritters.

BOHEMIAN

French impression came strongly about this time, and the Poodle Dog, of Paris, had its prototype at Bush and Dupont streets. This was one of the earliest of the type known as "French Restaurants," and numerous convivial parties of men and women found its private rooms convenient for rendezvous.

BIRTH OF THE
FRENCH
RESTAURANT

Old Pierre of later days, who was found dead out on the Colma road some two years after the fire of 1906, was a waiter at the Poodle Dog when it started, and by saving his tips and making good investments he was able to open a similar restaurant at Stockton and Market, which he called the Pup. The Pup was famous for its frogs' legs a la poulette. In this venture Pierre had a partner, to whom he sold out a few years later and then he opened the Tortoni in O'Farrell street, which became one of the most famous of the pre-fire restaurants, its table d'hote dinners being considered the best in the city. When Claus Spreckels built the tall Spreckels building Pierre and his partner opened the Call restaurant in the top stories. With the fire both of the restaurants went out of existence, and the old proprietor of the Poodle Dog having died, Pierre and a partner named Pon bought the place, and for a year or so after the fire it was one of the best French restaurants in the city. After Pierre's untimely death the restaurant was merged with Bergez and Frank's, and is now in Bush street above Kearny.

Much romance attached to Pierre, it being generally believed that he belonged to a wealthy French family, because of his education, his unfailing courtesy, his ready wit and his gentility. Pierre specialized in fish cooked with wine, and as a favor to his patrons he would go to the kitchen and prepare the dish with his own hands.

In O'Farrell street the Delmonico was one of the most famous of the French restaurants until the fire.

SAN FRANCISCO

BIRTH OF THE FRENCH RESTAURANT

It was several stories high, and each story contained private rooms. Carriages drove directly into the building from the street and the occupants went by elevator to soundproof rooms above, where they were served by discreet waiters.

The Poodle Dog, the Pup, Delmonico's, Jacques, Frank's, the Mint, Bergez, Felix and Campi's are the connecting links between the fire and the pioneer days. Some of them still carry the names and memories of the old days. All were noted for their good dinners and remarkably low prices.

Shortly after the fire Blanco, formerly connected with the old Poodle Dog, opened a place in O'Farrell street, between Hyde and Larkin, calling it "Blanco's." During the reconstruction period this was by far the best restaurant in the city, and it is still one of the noted places. Later Blanco opened a fine restaurant in Mason street, between Turk and Eddy, reviving the old name of the Poodle Dog, and here all the old traditions have been revived. Both of these savor of the old type of French restaurants, catering to a class of quiet spenders who carefully guard their indiscretions.

In the early '50s and '60s the most noted places were not considered respectable enough for ladies, and at restaurants like the Three Trees, in Dupont just above Bush street, ladies went into little private rooms through an alley. Peter Job saw his opportunity and opened a restaurant where special attention was paid to lady patrons, and shortly after the New York restaurant, in Kearny street, did the same.

Merging the post-pioneer era with the pre-fire era came the Maison Doree, which became famous in many ways. It was noted for oysters a la poulette, prepared after the following recipe:

One-half cup butter, three tablespoons flour, yolks of three eggs. One pint chicken stock (or veal), one tablespoonful

BOHEMIAN

OYSTERS A LA POULETTE

lemon juice, one-eighth teaspoon pepper, one level teaspoon salt. Beat the butter and flour together until smooth and white. Then add salt, pepper and lemon juice. Gradually pour boiling stock on this mixture and simmer for ten minutes. Beat the yolks of eggs in a saucepan, gradually pouring the cooked sauce upon them. Pour into a double boiler containing boiling water in lower part of utensil. Stir the mixture for one and one-half minutes. Into this put two dozen large oysters and let cook until edges curl up and serve hot.

Captain Cropper, an old Marylander, had a restaurant that was much patronized by good livers, and in addition to the usual Southern dishes he specialized on terrapin a la Maryland, sending back to his native State for the famous diamond-back terrapin. His recipe for this was as follows:

TERRAPIN A LA MARYLAND

Cut a terrapin in small pieces, about one inch long, after boiling it. Put the pieces in a saute pan with two ounces of sweet butter, salt, pepper, a very little celery salt, a pinch of paprika. Simmer for a few minutes and then add one glass of sherry wine, which reduce to half by boiling. Then add one cup of cream, bring to a boil and thicken with two yolks of eggs mixed with a half cup of cream. Let it come to a near boil and add half a glass of dry sherry and serve.

You may thicken the terrapin with the following mixture: Two raw yolks of eggs, two boiled yolks of eggs, one ounce of butter, one ounce corn starch. Rub together and pass through a fine sieve.

Uncle Tom's Cabin, Tony Oakes, the Hermitage, and Cornelius Stagg's were noted road-houses where fine meals were served, but these are scarcely to be considered as San Francisco Bohemian restaurants.

The Reception, on the corner of Sutter and Webb streets, which continued up to the time of the fire, was noted for its terrapin specialties, but it was rather malodorous and ladies who patronized it usually went in through the Webb street entrance to keep from being seen. The old Baldwin Hotel, which stood where the

SAN FRANCISCO

Flood building now stands, at the corner of Market and Powell, and which was destroyed by fire some fourteen years ago, was the favorite resort of many of the noted men of the West, and the grill had the distinction of being the best in San Francisco at that time. The grill of the Old Palace Hotel was also of highest order, and this was especially true of the Ladies' Grill which was then, as now, noted for its artistic preparation of a wondrous variety of good things.

BIRTH OF THE FRENCH RESTAURANT

Probably the most unique place of the pioneer and post-pioneer eras was the Cobweb Palace, at Meiggs's Wharf, run by queer old Abe Warner. It was a little ramshackle building extending back through two or three rooms filled with all manner of old curios such as comes from sailing vessels that go to different parts of the world. These curios were piled indiscriminately everywhere, and there were boxes and barrels piled with no regard whatever for regularity. This heterogeneous conglomeration was covered with years of dust and cobwebs, hence the name. Around and over these played bears, monkeys, parrots, cats, and dogs, and whatever sort of bird or animal that could be accommodated until it had the appearance of a small menagerie. Warner served crab in various ways and clams. In the rear room, which was reached by a devious path through the debris, he had a bar where he served the finest of imported liquors, French brandy, Spanish wines, English ale, all in the original wood. He served no ordinary liquor of any sort, saying that if anybody wanted whiskey they could get it at any saloon. He catered to a class of men who knew good liquors, and his place was a great resort for children, of whom he was fond and who went there to see the animals. The frontispiece of this book is from one of the few existing (if not the only one) photographs of the place.

BOHEMIAN

Equally unique, yet of higher standard, was the Palace of Art, run by the Hackett brothers, in Post street near Market. Here were some of the finest paintings and marble carvings to be found in the city, together with beautiful hammered silver plaques and cups. Curios of all sorts were displayed on the walls, and among them were many queer wood growths showing odd shapes as well as odd colorings. A large and ornate bar extended along one side of the immense room and tables were placed about the room and in a balcony that ran along one side. Here meals were served to both men and women, the latter being attracted by the artistic display and unique character of the place. This was destroyed by the fire and all the works of art lost.

BIRTH OF THE FRENCH RESTAURANT

SAN FRANCISCO

Three times destroyed by fire, and three times rebuilt, the Cliff House stands on a rocky promontory overlooking the Sundown Sea, where San Francisco's beach is laved by the waves of the Ocean. Since the first Cliff House was erected this has been a place famous the world over because of its scenic beauty and its overlooking the Seal Rocks, where congregate a large herd of sealions disporting much to the edification of the visitors. Appealing from its romantic surroundings, interesting because of its history, and attractive through its combination of dashing waves and beautiful beach extending miles in one direction, with the rugged entrance to Golden Gate in the other, with the mysterious Farallones in the dim distance, the Cliff House may well be classed as one of the great Bohemian restaurants of San Francisco.

AT THE CLIFF HOUSE

Lovers of the night life know it well for it is the destination of many an automobile party. During the day its terraces are filled with visitors from abroad who make this a part of their itinerary, and here, as they drink in the wondrous beauty of the scene spread before them, partake of well prepared and well served dishes such as made both the Cliff House and San Francisco well and favorably known and whose fame is not bounded by the continent.

But for a most pleasant visit to the Cliff House one should choose the early morning hours, and go out when the air is blowing free and fresh from the sea, the waves cresting with amber under the magic touch of the easterly sun. Select a table next to one of the western windows and order a breakfast that is served here better than any place we have tried. This breakfast will consist of broiled breast of young turkey, served with broiled Virginia ham with a side dish of corn fritters. When you sit down to this after a brisk ride out through Golden Gate Park, you have the great sauce, appetite,

BOHEMIAN

and with a pot of steaming coffee whose aroma rises like the incense to the Sea Gods, you will feel that while you have thought you had good breakfasts before this, you know that now you are having the best of them all. Of course there are many other good things to order if you like, but we have discovered nothing that makes so complete a breakfast as this.

AT THE
CLIFF
HOUSE

SAN FRANCISCO

"Is everybody happy? Oh, it is only nine o'clock and we've got all night." It was a clear, fresh young voice, full of the joy of living and came from a young woman whose carefree air seemed to say of her existence as of the night "We've got all life before us." The voice, the healthful face and vigorous form, the very live and joyous expression were all significant of the time and place. It was Sunday night and the place was Steve Sanguinetti's, with roysterers in full swing and every table filled and dozens of patrons waiting along the walls ready to take each seat as it was emptied. Here were young men and women just returned from their various picnics across the Bay to their one great event of the week—a Sunday dinner at Sanguinetti's.

SOME ITALIAN RESTAURANTS

Over in one corner of the stifling room, on a raised platform, sat two oily and fat negroes, making the place hideous with their ribald songs and the twanging of a guitar and banjo. When a familiar air was sounded the entire gathering joined in chorus, and when such tunes as "There'll Be a Hot Time in the Old Town Tonight" came, the place was pandemonium. Yet through it all perfect order was kept by the fat proprietor, his muscular "bouncer" and two policemen stationed at the doors. Noise was rather invited than frowned upon, and the only line drawn regarding conduct was the throwing of bread. Probably Steve did not want it wasted.

It was all free and easy and nobody took offense at anything said or done. In fact if one were squeamish about such things Sanguinetti's was no place for him or her. One found one's self talking and laughing with the people about as if they were old friends. It made no difference how you were dressed, nor how dignified you tried to be, it was all one with the crowd around the tables. If you wished to stay there in comfort you had

BOHEMIAN

SOME ITALIAN RESTAURANTS

to be one of them, and dignity had to be left outside or it would make you so uncomfortable that you would carry it out, to an accompaniment of laughter and jeers of the rest of the diners.

So far as eating was concerned that was not one of the considerations when discussing Sanguinetti's. It was a table d'hote dinner served with a bottle of "Dago red," for fifty cents. You gave the waiter a tip of fifteen cents or "two bits" as you felt liberal, and he was satisfied. If you were especially pleased you gave the darkeys ten cents, not because you enjoyed the music, but just "because."

The one merit of Sanguinetti's before the fire was the fact that all the regular customers were unaffected and natural. They came from the factories, canneries, shops, and drays, and after a week of heart-breaking work this was their one relaxation and they enjoyed it to the full. Many people from the residential part of the city, and many visitors at the hotels, went there as a part of slumming trips, but the real sentiment was expressed by the young girl when she sang out "Is everybody happy?"

Sanguinetti still has his restaurant, and there is still to be found the perspiring darkeys, playing and singing their impossible music, and a crowd still congregates there, but it is not the old crowd for this, like all things else in San Francisco, has changed, and instead of the old-time assemblage of young men and women whose lack of convention came from their natural environment, there is now a crowd of young and old people who patronize it because they have heard it is "so Bohemian."

Thrifty hotel guides take tourists there and tell them it is "the only real Bohemian restaurant in San Francisco," and when the outlanders see the antics of the

SAN FRANCISCO

people and listen to the ribald jests and bad music of the darkeys, they go back to their hotels and tell with bated breath of one of the most wonderful things they have ever seen, and it is one of the wonderful things of their limited experience.

SOME ITALIAN RESTAURANTS

Among the pre-fire restaurants of note were several Italian places which appealed to the Bohemian spirit through their good cooking and absence of conventionality, together with the inexpensiveness of the dinners. Among these were the Buon Gusto, the Fior d'Italia, La Estrella, Campi's and the Gianduja. Of these Campi's, in Clay street below Sansome, was the most noted, and the primitive style of serving combined with his excellent cooking brought him fame. All of these places, or at least restaurants with these names, are still in existence.

Jule's, the Fly Trap, the St. Germain and the Cosmos laid claim to distinction through their inexpensiveness, up to the time of the fire. All of these names are still to be seen over restaurants and they are still in that class, Jule's, possibly, being better than it was before the fire. A good dinner of seven or eight courses, well cooked and well served, could be had in these places for fifty cents. Lombardi's was of the same type but his price was but twenty-five cents for a course dinner in many respects the equal of the others.

Pop Floyd, recently killed by his bartender in an altercation, had a place down in California street much patronized by business men. He had very good service and the best of cooking, and for many years hundreds of business men gathered there at luncheon in lieu of a club. The place is still in existence and good service and good food is to be had there, but it has lost its Bohemian atmosphere.

In Pine street above Montgomery was the Viticultural, a restaurant that had great vogue owing to the

BOHEMIAN

excellence of its cooking. Its specialty was marrow on toast and broiled mushrooms, and game.

SOME ITALIAN RESTAURANTS

To speak of Bohemian San Francisco and say nothing of the old Hoffman saloon, on Second and Market streets, would be like the play of Hamlet with Hamlet left out. "Pop" Sullivan, or "Billy" Sullivan, according to the degree of familiarity of the acquaintance, boasted of the fact that from the day this place opened until he sold the doors were closed but once, the keys having been thrown away on opening day. During all the years of its existence the only day it was closed was the day of the funeral of Sullivan's mother. Here was the most magnificent bar in San Francisco, and in connection was a restaurant that catered to people who not only knew good things but ordered them. The back part of the place with entrance on Second street was divided off into little rooms with tables large enough for four. These rooms were most lavish in their decoration, the most interesting feature being that they were all made of different beautiful woods, highly polished. Woods were here from all parts of the world, each being distinctive. In these rooms guests were served with the best the market afforded, by discreet darkeys. This place was the best patronized of all the Bohemian resorts of the city up to the time of the fire. One of the special dainties served were the Hoffman House biscuits, light and flaky, such as could be found nowhere else.

Out by Marshall Square, by the City Hall, was Good Fellow's Grotto, started by Techau, who afterward built and ran the Techau Tavern. This place was in a basement and had much vogue among politicians and those connected with the city government. It specialized on beefsteaks.

Under the St. Ann building, at Eddy and Powell streets, was the Louvre, started and managed by Carl

SAN FRANCISCO

Zinkand, who afterward opened the place in Market above Fourth street, called Zinkand's. This was distinctly German in appointments and cooking and was the best of its kind in the city. Under the Phelan building at O'Farrell and Market was the Old Louvre in which place one could get German cooking, but it was not a place that appealed to those who knew good service.

SOME ITALIAN RESTAURANTS

Bab's had a meteoric career and was worthy of much longer life, but Babcock had too high an idealization of what San Francisco wanted. He emulated the Parisian restaurants in oddities, one of his rooms being patterned after the famous Cabaret de la Mort, and one dined off a coffin and was lighted by green colored tapers affixed to skulls. Aside from its oddities it was one of the best places for a good meal for Bab had the art of catering down to a nicety. There were rooms decorated to represent various countries and in each room you could get a dinner of the country represented.

Thompson's was another place that was too elaborate for its patronage and after a varied existence from the old Oyster Loaf to a cafeteria Thompson was compelled to leave for other fields and San Francisco lost a splendid restaurateur. He opened the place under the Flood building, after the fire, in most magnificent style, taking in two partners. The enormous expense and necessary debt contracted to open the place was too much and Thompson had to give up his interest. This place is now running as the Portola-Louvre.

Much could be written of these old-time restaurants, and as we write story after story amusing, interesting, and instructive come to mind, each indicative of the period when true Bohemianism was to be found in the City that Was.

An incident that occurred in the old Fior d'Italia well illustrates this spirit of camaraderie, as it shows

BOHEMIAN

the good-fellowship that then obtained. We went to that restaurant for dinner one evening, and the proprietor, knowing our interest in human nature studies, showed us to a little table in the back part of the room, where we could have a good view of all the tables. Our table was large enough to seat four comfortably, and presently, as the room became crowded, the proprietor, with many excuses, asked if he could seat two gentlemen with us. They were upper class Italians, exceedingly polite, and apologized profusely for intruding upon us. In a few minutes another gentleman entered and our companions at once began frantic gesticulations and called him to our table, where room was made and another cover laid. Again and again this occurred until finally at a table suited for four, nine of us were eating, laughing, and talking together, we being taken into the comradeship without question. When it came time for us to depart the entire seven rose and stood, bowing as we passed from the restaurant.

SOME ITALIAN RESTAURANTS

SAN FRANCISCO

Running through all the fabric of San Francisco's history is the thread of Mexican and Spanish romance and tradition, carrying us back to the very days when the trooper sent out by Portola first set eyes on the great inland sea now known as San Francisco Bay. It would seem that the cuisinaire most indelibly stamped on the taste of the old San Franciscan would, therefore, be of either Spanish or Mexican origin. That this is not a fact is because among the earliest comers to California after it passed from Mexican hands to those of the United States, were French and Italian cooks, and the bon vivants of both lands who wanted their own style of cooking. While the Spanish did not impress their cooking on San Francisco, it is the cuisine of the Latin races that has given to it its greatest gastronomic prestige, and there still remains from those very early days recipes of the famous dishes which had their beginnings either in Spain or Mexico.

IMPRESS OF MEXICO

There is much misconception regarding both Spanish and Mexican cooking, for it is generally accepted as a fact that all Mexican and Spanish dishes are so filled with red pepper as to be unpalatable to the normal stomach of those trained to what is called "plain American cooking." Certain dishes of Mexican and Spanish origin owe their fine flavor to discriminating use of chili caliente or chili dulce, but many of the best dishes are entirely innocent of either. The difference between Spanish and Mexican cooking is largely a matter of sentiment. It is a peculiarity of the Spaniard that he does not wish to be classed as a Mexican, and on the other hand the Mexican is angry if he be called a Spaniard. But the fact remains that their cooking is much alike, so much so, in fact, as to be indistinguishable except by different names for similar dishes, and frequently these are the same.

BOHEMIAN

The two famous and world-known dishes of this class of cooking are tortillas and tamales. It is generally supposed that both of these are the product of Mexico, but this is not the case. The tamale had its origin in Spain and was carried to Mexico by the conquistadors, and taken up as a national dish by the natives after many years. The tortilla, on the other hand, is made now exactly as it was made by the Mexican Indian when the Spanish found the country. The aborigine prepared his corn on a stone metate and made it into cakes by patting it with the hand, then cooked it on a hot stone before an open fire. It is still made in that manner in the heart of Mexico, and we could tell a story of how we saw this done one night in the midst of a dense tropical forest, while muleteers and mozas of a great caravan sat around their little camp-fires, whose fitful light served to intensify the weird appearance of the shadows of the Indians as they passed to and fro among their packs, but this is not the place for such stories.

Of the old Mexican restaurants, those of us who can look back to the days of a quarter of a century ago remember old Felipe and Maria, the Mexican couple who kept the little place in the alley back of the old county jail, off Broadway. Here one had to depend entirely upon sentiment, or rather sentimentality, to be pleased. The cooking was truly Mexican for it included the usual Mexican disregard for dirt. Chattering monkeys and parrots were hanging around the kitchen, peering into pots and fingering viands, and they served to attract attention from myriads of cockroaches that swarmed about the walls. One could go to this place just on the theory that one is willing to try anything once, but aside from its picturesque old couple, and its Dantesque appearance, it offered nothing to induce a return unless it was to entertain a friend.

IMPRESS OF MEXICO

SAN FRANCISCO

Everyone who lived in San Francisco before the fire remembers Ricardo, he of the one eye, who served so well at Luna's, on Vallejo and Dupont streets. Ricardo had but one eye but he could see the wants of his patrons much better than many of the later day waiters who have two.

IMPRESS OF MEXICO

Luna's brought fame to San Francisco and in more than one novel of San Francisco life it was featured. Entering the place one came into the home life of the Luna family, and reached the dining room through the parlor, where Mrs. Luna, busy with her drawn work, and all the little Lunas and the neighbors and their children foregathered in the window spaces behind the torn Nottingham curtains which partially concealed the interior from passers on the street. The elder sons and daughters attended to the wants of those who fancied any of the curios displayed in the long showcase that extended from the door to the rear of the room.

Passing through this family group one came to the curtained dining room proper, although there were a number of tables in the family parlor to be used in case of a rush of patrons. Luna's dinners were a feature of the old San Francisco. They were strictly Mexican, from the unpalatable soup (Mexicans do not understand how to make good soup) to the "dulce" served at the close of the meal. First came the appetizers in form of thin slices of salami and of a peculiar Mexican sausage, so extremely hot with chili pepino as to immediately call for a drink of claret to assauge the burning. Then came the soup which we experienced ones always passed over. The salad of modern tables was replaced by an enchilada, and then came either chili con carne or chili con pollo according to the day of the week, Sundays having as the extra attraction the chili con pollo, or chicken with pepper. In place of bread they served tortillas, which were rolled and used as a spoon

BOHEMIAN

or fork if one were so inclined. Following this was what is known among unenlightened as "stuffed pepper," but which is called by the Spanish, from which country it gets its name, "chili reinas." To signify the close of the meal came frijoles fritas or fried beans, and these were followed by the dessert consisting of some preserved fruit or of a sweet tamale. Fifty cents paid the bill and a tip of fifteen cents to Ricardo made him as happy and as profuse with his thanks as the present day waiter on receipt of half a dollar.

IMPRESS OF MEXICO

Accepting Luna's as the best type of the Mexican restaurant of the days before the fire, our inquiry developed the fact that the dish on which he specialized was chili reinas, and this is the recipe he used in their preparation:

CHILIS REINAS

Roast large bell peppers until the skin turns black. Wash in cold water and rub off the blackened skin. Cut around the stem and remove the seed and coarse veins. Take some dry Monterey cheese, grated fine, and with this fill the peppers, closing the end with a wooden toothpick.

Prepare a batter made as follows: Beat the yolks and whites of six eggs separately, then mix, and stir in a little flour to make a thin batter. Have a pan of boiling lard ready and after dipping the stuffed pepper into the batter dip it into the lard. Remove quickly and dip again in the batter and then again in the lard where it is to remain until fried a light, golden brown, keeping the peppers entirely covered with the boiling lard.

Take the seeds of the peppers, one small white onion and two tomatoes and grind all together into a pulp, add a little salt and let cook ten minutes. When the chilis are fried turn the remainder of the batter into the tomatoes and boil twenty minutes, then turn this sauce over the peppers.

This is a most delicious dish and can be varied by using finely ground meat to stuff the peppers instead of the cheese.

Mexican restaurants of the present day in San Francisco are a delusion, and unsatisfactory.

SAN FRANCISCO

Much has been said and more printed regarding San Francisco's Barbary Coast—much of truth and much mythical. Probably no other individual district has been so instrumental in giving to people of other parts of the country an erroneous idea of San Francisco. It is generally accepted as a fact that in Barbary Coast Vice flaunted itself in reckless abandon before the eyes of the world, showing those things usually concealed behind walls and under cover of the darkness. According to the purists here youth of both sexes was debauched, losing both money and souls. To speak of seeing Barbary Coast brought furtive looks and lowered voices, as if contamination even from the thought were possible. No slumming party was completed without a visit to the "Coast," after Chinatown's manufactured horrors had been shuddered at.

One cannot well speak of the Barbary Coast without bringing into consideration the Social Evil, for here was concentrated dozens of the poor unfortunates of the underworld, compelled to eke out miserable existence through playing on the foibles and vanities of men, or seek oblivion in a suicide's grave. We do not propose to discuss this phase of Barbary Coast as that is not a part of Bohemianism.

We have visited the Coast many times, at all hours of the night, and beyond the unconcealed license of open caresses we have seen nothing shocking to our moral sense that equalled what we have seen in Broadway, New York, or in some of the most fashionable hotels and restaurants of San Francisco on New Year's Eve. Dancing, singing and music—all that is embodied in the "wine, women and song" of the poets, was to be found there, but it was open, and had none of the veiled suggestion to be found in places considered among the best.

BOHEMIAN

In Barbary Coast we have seen more beautiful dancing than on any stage, or in the famous Moulin Rouge, or Jardin Mabile of Paris. In fact, many of the modern dances that have become the vogue all over the country, even being carried to Europe, had their origin in Pacific street dance halls. Texas Tommy, the Grizzly Bear, and many others were first danced here, and some of the finest Texas Tommy dancers on eastern stages went from the dance halls of San Francisco's Barbary Coast.

ON THE
BARBARY
COAST

Vice was there—yes. It was open—yes. But there was the attraction of light and life and laughter that drew crowds nightly.

Barbary Coast was a part of San Francisco's Bohemianism because of its unconventionality, for, you know, there is conventionality even in Vice. Here was the rendezvous of sailormen from all parts of the world, for here they found companionship and joviality.

Up to the time of the closing of Barbary Coast molestation of women on the streets of San Francisco was almost unheard of. Since its closing it is becoming more and more hazardous for women to walk alone at night in the only large city in the world that always had the reputation of guarding its womankind.

SAN FRANCISCO

Times change and we change with them is well evidenced by the restaurant life of the present day San Francisco. Now, as before the fire, we have the greatest restaurant city of the world—a city where home life is subordinated to the convenience of apartment dwelling and restaurant meals—but the old-time Bohemian finds neither the same atmosphere nor the same restaurants.

THE CITY THAT WAS PASSES

True, many of the old names have been retained or revived, but there is not felt the old spirit of camaraderie. Old personalities have passed away and old customs have degenerated. Those who await The Call feel that with the passing of the old city there passed much that made life worth living, and as they prepare to cross to the Great Beyond, they live in their memories of the Past.

With reverence we think of the men and women of the early San Francisco—those who made the city the Home of Bohemia—and it is with this feeling that we now come to discuss the Bohemian restaurants of the New San Francisco.

BOHEMIAN

SANG THE SWAN SONG

In the latter part of April, 1906, when the fire-swept streets presented their most forbidding aspect, and when the only moving figures to be seen after nightfall were armed soldiers guarding the little remaining of value from depredations of skulking vagabonds, a number of the old Bohemian spirits gathered at the corner of Montgomery and Commercial streets, and gazed through the shattered windows into the old dining room where they had held many a royal feast. On the blackened walls might still be seen scarred pictures, fringed by a row of black cats along the ceiling. They turned their steps out toward the Presidio, hunted among the Italian refugees and there found Coppa—he of the wonderful black cats, and it took little persuasion to induce him to go back to his ruined restaurant and prepare a dinner, such as had made his place famous among artists, writers, and other Bohemians, in the days when San Francisco was care-free and held her arms wide open in welcome to all the world.

It was such a dinner as has been accorded to few. Few there are who have the heart to make merry amid crumbling ruins of all they held dear in the material world. The favored ones who assembled there will always hold that dinner in most affectionate memory, and to this day not one thinks of it without the choking that comes from over-full emotion. It was more than a tribute to the days of old—it marked the passing of the old San Francisco and the inauguration of the new.

It was Bohemia's Swan Song, sung by those to whom San Francisco held more than pleasure—more than sentimentality. It held for them close-knit ties that nothing less than a world-shaking cataclysm could sever—and the cataclysm had arrived.

The old Coppa restaurant in Montgomery street became a memory and on its ashes came the new one,

SAN FRANCISCO

located in Pine street between Montgomery and Kearny streets, and for a number of years this remained the idol of Bohemia until changed conditions drove the tide of patronage far up toward Powell, Ellis, Eddy and O'Farrell streets. At that time there grew up a mushroom crop of so-called restaurants in Columbus avenue close to Barbary Coast such as Caesar's, the Follies Cabaret, Jupiter and El Paradiso, where space was reserved in the middle of the floor for dancing. Coppa emulated the new idea by fitting out a gorgeous basement room at the corner of Kearny and Jackson, which he called the Neptune Palace. It represented a great grotto under the ocean, and here throngs gathered nightly to dance and eat until the police commissioners closed all of these resorts, as well as Barbary Coast.

SANG THE SWAN SONG

Coppa became financially injured by this venture and was forced to take a partner in his old restaurant, and finally gave up his share and went beyond the city limits and opened the Pompeiian Garden, on the San Mateo road, and there with his heroic little wife tried to rebuild his shrunken fortunes, leaving the historic restaurant with its string of black cats and its memorable pictures on the walls to less skilled hands. He struggled against hard times and at the time of this writing he, with his wife, their son and his wife, are giving the old-time dinners and trying to make the venture a success.

In the old days it was considered a feat of gormandizing to go through one of Coppa's dinners and eat everything set before you for one dollar. Notwithstanding the delicious dishes he prepared and the wonderful recipes, the quantity served was so great that one would have to be possessed of enormous capacity, indeed, to be able to say at the end of the meal that he had eaten all that was given him.

BOHEMIAN

In his Pompeiian Garden Coppa still maintains his old reputation for most tasty viands and liberal portions, and if one desire to find the true Bohemian restaurant of San Francisco today, one that approaches the old spirit of the days before the fire, he need but go out to Coppa's and while he will not have his eyes regaled by the quaint drawings with which the old-time artists decorated the walls, nor the hurrying footsteps along the ceiling to the famous center table where sat some of the world's most notable Bohemians on their visits to San Francisco, nor the frieze of black cats around the cornice, nor the Bohemian verse, written under inspiration of "Dago red," he will find the same old cooking, done by Coppa himself.

SANG THE SWAN SONG

We asked Coppa what he considered his best dish and he gave us the Irishman's reply by asking another question:

"What do you think of it?"

There are so many to choose from that our answer was difficult but we finally stopped at "Chicken Portola." It was then that the old smile came back to Coppa's face.

"Ah! Chicken Portola. That is my own idea. It is the most delicious way chicken was ever cooked."

This is the recipe as Coppa gave it to us, his little wife standing at his side and giving, now and then, a suggestion as Coppa's memory halted:

CHICKEN PORTOLA A LA COPPA

Take a fresh cocoanut and cut off the top, removing nearly all of the meat. Put together three tablespoonfuls of chopped cocoanut meat and two ears of fresh, green corn, taken from the cob. Slice two onions into four tablespoonfuls of olive oil, together with a tablespoonful of diced bacon fried in olive oil, add one chopped green pepper, half a dozen tomatoes stewed with salt and pepper, one clove of garlic, and cook all together until it thickens. Strain this into the corn and

SAN FRANCISCO

cocoanut and add one spring chicken cut in four pieces. Put the mixture into the shell of the cocoanut, using the cut-off top as a cover, and close tightly with a covering of paste around the jointure to keep in the flavors. Put the cocoanut into a pan with water in it and set in the oven, well heated, for one hour, basting frequently to prevent the cocoanut's burning.

SANG
THE SWAN
SONG

A bare recital of the terms of the recipe cannot bring to the uninitiated even a suspicion of the delightful aroma that comes from the cocoanut when its top is lifted, nor can it give the slightest idea of the delicacy of the savor arising from the combination of the cocoanut with young chicken. It is not a difficult dish to prepare, and if you cannot get it at any of the restaurants, and we are sure you cannot, try it at home some time and surprise your friends with a dish to be found in only one restaurant in the world. If you desire it at Coppa's on your visit to San Francisco you will have to telephone out to him in advance (unless he has succeeded in getting back to the city, which he contemplates) so that he can prepare it for you, and, take our word for it, you will never regret doing so.

Coppa has many wonderful dishes to serve, and he delights so much in your appreciation that he is always fearful something is wrong if you fail to do full justice to his meal. He showed this one evening when he had filled a little party of us to repletion by his lavish provision for our entertainment, and nature rebelled against anything more. To us came Coppa in tears.

"What is the matter with the chicken, Doctor? Is it not cooked just right?"

It was with difficulty that we made him understand that there was a limit to capacity, and that he had fed us with such bountiful hand we could eat no more. Even now when we go to Coppa's we have a little feeling of fear lest we offend him by not eating enough to convince him that we are pleased.

BOHEMIAN

Coppa's walls were always adorned with strange conceits of the artists and writers who frequented his place, and after a picture, or a bit of verse had remained until it was too familiar some one erased it and replaced it with something he thought was better. We preserved one written by an unknown Bohemian. We give it just as it was:

SANG
THE SWAN
SONG

> Through the fog of centuries, dim and dense,
> I sometimes seem to see
> The shadowy line of a back-yard fence
> And a feline shape of me.
> I hear the growl, and yowl and howl
> Of each nocturnal fight,
> And the throaty stir, half cry, half purr
> Of passionate delight,
> As seeking an amorous rendezvous
> My ancient brothers go stealing
> Through the purple gloom of night.
>
> I've seen your eyes, with a greenish glint;
> You move with a feline grace;
> And when you are pleased I catch the hint
> Of a purr in your throat and face.
> Then I wonder if you are dreaming, too,
> Of temples along the Nile,
> Where you yowled and howled, and loved and prowled,
> With many a sensuous wile,
> And borrowed the grace you own today
> From that other life in the far-away;
> And if such dreams beguile.
>
> I know that you sit by your cozy fire,
> When shadows crowd the room,
> And my soul responds to an old desire
> To roam through the velvety gloom,
> So stealthily stealing, softly shod,
> My spirit is hurrying thence
> To the lure of an ancient mystic god,
> Whose magnet is intense,
> Where I know your soul, too, roams in fur,
> For I hear it call with a throaty purr,
> From the shadowy back-yard fence.

SAN FRANCISCO

San Francisco's care-free spirit was fully exemplified before the ashes of the great fire of 1906 were cold. On every hand one could find little eating places established in the streets, some made of abandoned boxes, others of debris from the burned buildings, and some in vacant basements and little store rooms, while a few enterprising individuals improvised wheeled dining rooms and went from one part of the city to another serving meals.

BOHEMIA OF THE PRESENT

The vein of humor of irrepressible effervescence of spirit born of Bohemianism gave to these eating places high sounding names, and many were covered with witty signs which laughed in the face of Fate.

Fillmore became the great business street of the city now in ashes, and here were established the first restaurants of any pretensions, the Louvre being first to open an establishment that had the old-time appearance. This was on the corner of Fillmore and Ellis, and had large patronage, it being crowded nightly with men and women who seemed to forget that San Francisco had been destroyed. Thompson opened a large restaurant in O'Farrell street, just above Fillmore, and for two years or more did a thriving business, his place being noted for its good cooking and its splendid service. One of his waiters, Phil Tyson, was one of the earlier ones to go back into the burned district to begin business and he opened a restaurant called the Del Monte in Powell street near Market, but it was too early for success and closed after a short career.

Thompson enlisted others to join with him in opening a magnificent place under the new Flood building at the gore of Powell and Market street, but through faulty understanding of financial power Thompson was compelled to give up his interest and the place afterward closed. It has since been reopened under the name of the Portola-Louvre, where now crowds assem-

41

BOHEMIAN

BOHEMIA OF THE PRESENT

ble nightly to listen to music and witness cabaret performances. Here, as well as in a number of other places, one can well appreciate the colloquial definition of "cabaret." That which takes the rest out of restaurant and puts the din in dinner. If one likes noise and distraction while eating such places are good to patronize.

Across the street from the Portola-Louvre at 15 Powell street is the modernized Techau Tavern now known as "Techau's". Here there is always good music and food well cooked and well served, and always a lively crowd during the luncheon, dinner and after-theatre hours. The room is not large but its dimensions are greatly magnified owing to the covering of mirrors which line the walls. This garish display of mirrors, and elaborate decoration of ceiling and pillars, gives it the appearance of the abode of Saturnalia, but decorum is the rule among the patrons.

Around at 168 O'Farrell street, just opposite the Orpheum theatre, is Tait-Zinkand restaurant, or as it is more popularly known, "Tait's". John Tait is the presiding spirit here, he having made reputation as club manager, and then as manager of the Cliff House. One of the partners here was Carl Zinkand, who ran the old Zinkand's before the fire.

While these three restaurants are of similar type neither has the pre-fire atmosphere. They are lively, always, with music and gay throngs, and serve good food.

One of the early restaurants established after the fire was Blanco's, at 857 O'Farrell street, and later Blanco opened the Poodle Dog in Mason street just above Eddy. Both of these restaurants are of the old French type and are high class in every respect. The Poodle Dog has a hotel attachment where one may get rooms or full apartments.

SAN FRANCISCO

If you know how to order, and do not care to count the cost when you order, probably the best dinner at these restaurants can be had at either Blanco's or the Poodle Dog. The cuisine is of the best and the chefs rank at the top of their art. Prices are higher than at the other restaurants mentioned, but one certainly gets the best there is prepared in the best way.

BOHEMIA OF THE PRESENT

But the same food, prepared equally well, is to be found in a number of less pretentious places. At the two mentioned one pays for the surroundings as well as for the food, and sometimes this is worth paying for.

The restaurants of the present day that approach nearest the old Bohemian restaurants of pre-fire days, of the French class, are Jack's in Sacramento street between Montgomery and Kearny; Felix, in Montgomery street between Clay and Washington, and the Poodle Dog-Bergez-Franks, in Bush street between Kearny and Grant avenue. In either of these restaurants you will be served with the best the market affords, cooked "the right way." In Clay street opposite the California Market is the New Frank's, one of the best of the Italian restaurants, and much patronized by Italian merchants. Next to it is Coppa's, but it is no longer run by Coppa. In this same district is the Mint, in Commercial street between Montgomery and Kearny streets. It has changed from what it was in the old days, but is still an excellent place to dine.

Negro's, at 625 Merchant street, near the Hall of Justice, has quite a following of those whose business attaches them to the courts, and while many claim this to be one of the best of its class, we believe the claim to be based less on good cooking than on the fact that the habitues are intimate, making it a pleasant resort for them. The cooking is good and the variety what the market affords.

BOHEMIAN

In Washington street, just off Columbus avenue, is Bonini's Barn, making great pretense through an unique idea. So far as the restaurant is concerned the food is a little below the average of Italian restaurants. One goes there once through curiosity and finds himself in a room that has all the appearance of the interior of a barn, with chickens and pigeons strutting around, harness hanging on pegs, and hay in mangers, and all the farming utensils around to give it the verisimilitude of country. Tables and chairs are crude in the extreme and old-time lanterns are used for lighting. It is an idea that is worth while, but, unfortunately, the proprietors depend too much on the decorative feature and too little on the food and how they serve it.

BOHEMIA OF THE PRESENT

The Fly Trap, and Charlie's Fashion, the first in Sutter street near Kearny and the other in Market near Sutter, serve well-cooked foods, especially soup, salads, and fish. Of course these are not the entire menus but of all the well-prepared dishes these are their best. Felix, mentioned before, also makes a specialty of his family soup, which is excellent.

Spanish dinners of good quality are to be had at the Madrilena, at 177 Eddy street, and at the Castilian, at 344 Sutter street. Both serve good Spanish dinners at reasonable prices. They serve table d'hote dinners, but you can also get Spanish dishes on special order.

Under the Monadnock building, in Market street near Third, is Jule's, well liked and well patronized because of its good cooking and good service. Jule is one of the noted restaurateurs of the city, having attained high celebrity before the fire. His prices are moderate and his cooking and viands of the best, and will satisfy the most critical of the gourmets.

At the corner of Market and Eddy streets is the Odeon, down in a basement, with decorations of most

SAN FRANCISCO

garish order. There is a good chef and the place has quite a vogue among lovers of good things to eat. Probably at no place in San Francisco can one find game cooked better than at Jack's, 615 Sacramento street. His ducks are always cooked so as to elicit high praise. He has an old-style French table d'hote dinner which he serves for $1.25, including wine. Or you may order anything in the market and you will find it cooked "the best way." One of the specialties of Jack's is fish, for which the restaurant is noted. It is always strictly fresh and cooked to suit the most fastidious taste.

BOHEMIA OF THE PRESENT

BOHEMIAN

AS IT IS IN GERMANY

When you see August (do not fail to pronounce it Owgoost) in repose you involuntarily say, that is if you understand German, "Mir ist alles an," which is the German equivalent of "I should worry." When August is in action you immediately get a thirst that nothing but a stein of cold beer will quench. August is the pride of the Heidelberg Inn at 35 Ellis street. All you can see from the street as you pass around the corner from Market, is a sign and some stairs leading down into a basement, but do not draw back just because it is a basement restaurant, for if you do you will miss one of the very few real Bohemian restaurants of San Francisco. Possibly our point of view will not coincide with that of others, but while there are dozens of other Bohemian restaurants there is but one Heidelberg Inn. Here is absolute freedom from irksome conventionality of other people, and none of the near Bohemianism of so many places claiming the title.

At the Heidelberg Inn one need never fear obtrusiveness on the part of other visitors, for here everybody attends strictly to his or her own party, enjoying a camaraderie that has all the genuine, whole-souled companionship found only where German families are accustomed to congregate to seek relaxation from the toil and worry of the day.

An evening spent in Heidelberg Inn is one replete with character study that cannot be excelled anywhere in San Francisco—and this means that everybody there is worth while as a study, from the little, bald-headed waiter, Heine, and the big, imposing waiter, August, to the "Herr Doctor" who comes to forget the serious surgical case that has been worrying him at the hospital. Here you do not find obtrusive waiters brushing imaginary crumbs from your chair with obsequious hand, nor over zealous stewards solicitous of your food's qual-

SAN FRANCISCO

ity. It is all perfect because it is made perfect by good management. Here are German families, from Grossfader and Grossmutter, down to the newest grandchild, sitting and enjoying their beer and listening to such music as can be heard nowhere else in San Francisco, as they eat their sandwiches of limburger, or more dainty dishes according to their tastes.

AS IT IS IN GERMANY

One can almost imagine himself in one of the famous rathskellers of Old Heidelberg—not at the Schloss, of course, for here you cannot look down on the Weiser as it flows beneath the windows of the great wine stube on the hill. But you have the real atmosphere, and this is enhanced by the mottoes in decoration and the flagons, steins and plaques that adorn the pillars as well as typical German environment.

It is when the martial strains of "De Wacht am Rhein" are heard from the orchestra, which of itself is an institution, that the true camaraderie of the place is appreciated, for then guests, waiters, barkeepers, and even the eagle-eyed, gray-haired manager, join in the swelling chorus, and you can well understand why German soldiers are inspired to march to victory when they hear these stirring chords.

But there is other music—sometimes neither inspiring nor beautiful when heard in a German rathskeller—the music of rag time. If there is anything funnier than a German orchestra trying to play rag-time music we have never heard it. It is unconscious humor on part of the orchestra, consequently is all the more excruciating.

But if you really love good music—music that has melody and rhythm and soothing cadences, go to the Heidelberg Inn and listen to the concert which is a feature of the place every evening. And while you are listening to the music you can enjoy such food as is to

BOHEMIAN

be found nowhere else in San Francisco, for it is distinctly Heidelbergian. We asked for the recipe that they considered the very best in the restaurant, and Hirsch, with a shrug of his shoulders, said: "Oh, we have so many fine dishes." We finally got him to select the one prized above all others and this is what Chef Scheiler gave us:

AS IT IS
IN
GERMANY

GERMAN
SAUER
BRATEN

Take four pounds of clear beef, from either the shoulder or rump, and pickle it for two days in one-half gallon of claret and one-half gallon of good wine vinegar (not cider). To the pickle add two large onions cut in quarters, two fresh carrots and about one ounce of mixed whole allspice, black peppers, cloves and bay leaves.

When ready for cooking take the meat out of the brine and put in a roasting pan. Put in the oven and brown to a golden color. Then take it out of the roasting pan and put it into a casserole, after sprinkling it with two ounces of flour. Put into the oven again and cook for half an hour, basting frequently with the original brine.

When done take the meat out of the sauce. Strain the sauce through a fine collander and add a few raisins, a piece of honey cake, or ginger snaps and the meat of one fresh tomato. Season with salt and pepper and a little sugar to taste. Slice and serve with the sauce over it.

For those who like German dishes and German cooking it is not necessary to confine yourself to the Heidelberg Inn, for both the Hof Brau, in Market just above Fourth street, and the German House Rathskeller, at Turk and Polk streets are good places where you can get what you want. The Hof Brau, however, is less distinctively German as the greater number of its patrons are Americans. The specialty of the Hof Brau is abalones, and they have as a feature this shell fish cooked in several ways. They also have as the chef in charge of the abalone dishes, Herbert, formerly chef for one of the yacht clubs of the coast, who claims to have the only proper recipe for making abalones tender.

SAN FRANCISCO

Under ordinary circumstances the abalone is tough and unpalatable, but after the deft manipulation of Herbert they are tender and make a fine dish, either fried, as chowder or a la Newberg. In addition to abalones the Hof Brau makes a specialty of little Oregon crawfish. While there is a distinctive German atmosphere at the Rathskeller of the German House, the place is too far out to gather such numbers as congregate at either the Heidelberg or the Hof Brau, but one can get the best of German cooking here and splendid service, and for a quiet little "Dutch supper" we know of no place that will accommodate you better than the Rathskeller.

On special occasions, when some German society or club is giving a dance or holding a meeting at the German House, the Rathskeller is the most typical German place in San Francisco, and if you go at such a time you will get all the "atmosphere" you will desire, as well as the best the market affords in the way of good viands.

AS IT IS
IN
GERMANY

BOHEMIAN

IN THE HEART
OF
ITALY

What a relief it is sometimes to have a good waiter say: "You do not know what you want? Will you let me bring you the best there is in the house?" Sometimes, you know, you really do not know what you want, and usually when that is the case you are not very hungry. That is always a good time to try new things. It is also possible that you do not know what you want because you do not know how to order. In either instance our advice is, if the waiter gets confidential and offers his assistance you will certainly miss something if you do not accept his good offices.

This was the case with us, one day when we were over at 1549 Stockton street, near Washington Square, at the Gianduja. The proper pronunciation of this is as if it were spelled Zhan-du-ya. This is one of the good Italian restaurants of the Latin quarter. At the Gianduja you get the two prime essentials to a good meal—good cooking and excellent service. It matters not whether you take their thirty-five cent luncheon or order a most elaborate meal, you will find that the service is just what it ought to be. We asked Brenti what he considered his most famous dish, and like all other proprietors, he shrugged his shoulders and said, with hands emphasizing his words:

"We have so many fine dishes."

"Of course we know that, but what do you consider the very best?"

"There is no one the 'very best'. I could give you two."

"Let it be two, then," was our immediate rejoinder, and here is what he gave us as the best recipes of the Gianduja.

First, let us give you an idea of the difficulty under which we secured these recipes by printing them just as he wrote them down for us, and then we shall elaborate

50

SAN FRANCISCO

a little and show the result of skillful questioning. This is the way he wrote the recipe for Risotto Milanaise:

RISOTTO A LA MILANAISE

"Onions chop fine—marrow and little butter—rice—saffron—chicken broth—wen cook add fresh butter and Parmesan cheese seasoned.

What was embodied in the words "wen cook" was the essential of the recipe and here is the way we got it:

Chop one large onion fine. Cut a beef marrow into small dice and stir it with the chopped onion. Put a small piece of butter in a frying pan and into this put the onion and marrow and fry to a delicate brown. Now add one scant cup of rice, stirring constantly, and into this put a pinch of saffron that has been bruised. When the rice takes on a brown color add, slowly, chicken broth as needed, until the rice is thoroughly cooked. Then add a lump of fresh butter about the size of a walnut, and sprinkle liberally with grated Parmesan cheese, seasoning to taste with pepper and salt. This is to be served with chicken or veal.

The second recipe was for Fritto Misto, and he wrote it as follows:

FRITTO MISTO

"Lamb chops and brains breaded—sweetbreads—escallop of veal—fresh mushrooms—Italian squash when in season—asparagus or cauliflower—fried in fresh butter—dipped in beaten eggs—lime jus."

"Fritto Misto" means fried mixture, and the recipe as we finally elucidated it is as follows:

Take a lamb chop, a piece of calf brain, one sweetbread, a slice of veal, a fresh mushroom, sliced Italian squash, a piece of asparagus or of cauliflower and dip these into a batter made of an egg well beaten with a little flour. Sprinkle these with a little lime juice and fry to a delicate brown in butter, adding salt and pepper to taste.

At the Gianduja, as at all other Italian restaurants not much affected by Americans, you will find an atmosphere of unconventionality that is delightful to the Bohemian. There is no irksome espionage on the part

BOHEMIAN

IN THE HEART OF ITALY

of other patrons, all of whom are there for the purpose of attending strictly to their own business, and the affairs of other diners are of no consequence to them. There is freedom of expression and unconsciousness, most pleasing after having experienced those other restaurants where it seems to be the business of all the rest of the guests to know just what you are eating and drinking. There is little of the obnoxious posing that one finds in restaurants of the down-town districts, for while Italians, in common with all other Latins, are natural born poseurs, they are not offensive in it, but rather impress you with the same feeling as the antics of a child.

One of the little, out-of-the way restaurants of the Italian quarter is the Leon d'Oro, at 1525 Grant avenue, and it is one of the surprises of that district. Lazzarini, he with the big voice, presides over the tiny kitchen in the rear of the room devoted to public service and family affairs. Soft-voiced Rita, with her demure air and her resemblance to Evangeline, with her crossed apron strings and delicate features, takes your order, and soon comes the booming sound from the neighborhood of the range, that announces to all patrons, as well as to some who may be in the vicinity on the street, that your order is ready, and then everybody knows what you are eating. As you sit, either in curtained alcove or at the common table in the main room, little Andrea will visit you with his cat. Both are institutions of the place and one is prone to wonder how a cat can have so much patience with a little boy. Andrea speaks Italian so fluently and so rapidly that it gives you the impression of a quick rushing stream of pure water, tumbling over the stones of a steep declivity. He is not yet old enough to understand that it is not everybody who knows how to speak Italian, but that makes not the slightest difference with him, for he talks without ever expecting an answer.

SAN FRANCISCO

Lazzarini understands the art and science of cooking, and some of the dishes he prepares are so unusual that one goes again and again to partake of them: Possibly his best dish is the following:

CHICKEN A LA LEON D'ORO

Cut a spring chicken into pieces. Place these in a pan containing hot olive oil, and season with salt and pepper. Turn the chicken until it is thoroughly browned, and add finely chopped green peppers. Let it cook awhile then add a finely chopped clove of garlic and a little sage. Put in a small glass of Marsala wine, tomato sauce and French mushrooms and let simmer for ten minutes. Before taking from the pan add half a tablespoonful of butter and serve on a hot plate.

Lazzarini also makes a specialty of snails, and they are well worth trying while you are experimenting with the unusual things to eat. The recipe for these is as follows:

SNAILS A LA BORDELAISE

Put ten pounds of snails in a covered barrel and keep for ten days. Then put in a tub with a handful of salt and a quarter of a gallon of vinegar. Stir for twenty minutes until a foam rises, then take out and wash thoroughly until the water runs clear. Put in a large pot a pint of virgin olive oil, four large onions and eight cloves of garlic, all chopped fine, and a small bunch of parsley, chopped fine. Put the pot over the fire and when the onions are browned stir in some white wine or Marsala and then put in the snails. Cover and let simmer for thirty-five minutes. While cooking add a pint of meat stock, a little butter and some anise seed. When done put in a soup tureen and serve. To remove the snails use small wooden toothpicks.

BOHEMIAN

San Francisco's world-famed Chinatown, like the rest of the city, is changed since the big fire, and the Chinatown of today is but a reminiscence of the old Oriental city that was set in the midst of the most thriving Occidental metropolis—The City That Was. There has never been much of Chinatown that savored of Bohemianism, but it has always been the vogue for visitors to make a trip through its mysterious alleys, peering into the fearsome dark doorways, listening to the ominous slamming doors of the "clubs," and shuddering in a delightful horror at the recumbent opium smokers, pointed out to them by the industrious guide. And when they were taken into one of the gambling houses and shown the double doors, and the many contrivances used to prevent police interference with the innocent games of fan tan and then were shown the secret underground passage leading from one of the gambling houses to the stage of the great Chinese theatre, two blocks away, they went home ready to believe anything told them about "the ways that are dark and tricks that are vain," for they were sure "the heathen Chinee was peculiar."

A BREATH OF THE ORIENT

Chinese restaurant life never appealed to Bohemians, and when it became necessary to entertain visitors with a trip to a Chinatown restaurant the ordinary service was of tea and rice cakes, served from lacquered trays, in gaudy rooms, and the admiring visitors could well imagine themselves in "far off Cathay."

Then came the fire and Chinatown, with the rest of the down-town portion of San Francisco, passed away. In the rebuilding the owners of the properties concluded to give the quarter a more Chinese aspect and pagoda-like structures are now to be found in all parts of the section. The curiosity of the tourist is an available asset to Chinatown, and with queer houses and queerer articles on sale there is always plenty of uninitiated to

SAN FRANCISCO

keep the guides busy, but from a city of more than twenty-five thousand Orientals in the midst of an enlightened city—an Asiatic city that had its own laws and executed its criminals with the most utter disregard for American laws, it has changed into one of the most law-abiding parts of the great city. With the passing of the queue came the adoption of the American style of dressing, and much of the picturesqueness of the old Chinatown has disappeared.

A BREATH OF THE ORIENT

But with the changed conditions there has come a change in the restaurant life of the quarter, and now a number of places have been opened to cater to Americans, and on every hand one sees "chop suey" signs, and "Chinese noodles." It goes without saying that one seldom sees a Chinaman eating in the restaurants that are most attractive to Americans. Some serve both white and yellow and others serve but the Chinese, and a few favored white friends.

Probably the best restaurant in Chinatown is that of the Hang Far Low Company, at 723 Grant avenue. Here is served such a variety of strange dishes that one has to be a brave Bohemian, indeed, to partake without question. Ordinarily when Chinese restaurants are mentioned but two dishes are thought of—chop suey and chow main. But neither is considered among the fine dishes served to Chinese epicures. It is much as if one of our best restaurants were to advertise hash as its specialty. Both these dishes might be termed glorified hash. The ingredients are so numerous and so varied with occasion that one is tempted to imagine them made of the table leavings, and that is not at all pleasant to contemplate.

We asked one of the managers at the Hang Far Low what he would order if he wished to get the best dish prepared in the restaurant, and he was even more em-

BOHEMIAN

phatic in his shrugs than the French or Italian managers. He protested that there were so many good things it was impossible to name just one as being the best. "You see, we have fish fins, they are very good. Snails, China style. Very good, too. Then we have turtle brought from China, different from the turtle they have here, and we cook it China style. Eels come from China and they are cooked China style, too. What is China style? That I cannot tell you for the cook knows and nobody else. When we cook China style everything is more better. We have here the very best tea."

A BREATH OF THE ORIENT

This may be taken as a sample of what to expect when visiting Chinatown's restaurants, and while we confess to having some excellent dishes served us in Chinatown, our preference lies in other paths of endeavor. We suppose it is all in the point of view, and our point of view is that there is nothing except superficiality in the ordinary Chinese restaurants frequented by Americans, and those not so frequented are impossible because of the average Chinaman's disregard for dirt and the usual niceties of food preparation.

SAN FRANCISCO

We wish it were in our power to describe a certain dinner as served us in a Japanese restaurant in the days that followed the great fire. Desiring to observe in fitting manner a birthday anniversary, we asked a Japanese friend if he could secure admission for a little party at a restaurant noted for serving none but the highest class Japanese. We did not even know where the restaurant was but had heard of such a place, and when we received word that we would be permitted to have a dinner there we invited a newspaper friend who was in the city from New York, together with two other friends and the Japanese, who was the editor of the Soko Shimbun. He took us to a dwelling house in O'Farrell street, having given previous notice of our coming. There was nothing on the outside to indicate that it was anything but a residence, but when we were ushered into the large front room, we found it beautifully decorated with immense chrysanthemums, and glittering with silver and cut glass on a magnificently arranged table.

ARTISTIC JAPAN

In deference to the fact that all but our Japanese friend were unaccustomed to chopsticks, forks were placed on the table as well as the little sticks that the Orientals use so deftly. At each place was a beautiful lacquer tray, about twelve by eighteen inches, a pair of chopsticks, a fork and a teaspoon. Before the meal was over several of us became quite expert in using the chopsticks.

When we were seated in came two little Japanese women, in full native costume, bearing a service of tea. The cups and saucers were of a most delicate blue and white ware, with teapot to match. Our first cup was taken standing in deference to a Japanese custom where all drank to the host. Then followed saki in little artistic bottles and saki cups that hold not much more than a double tablespoonful. Saki is the Japanese wine

BOHEMIAN

made of rice, and is taken in liberal quantities. At each serving some one drank to some one else, then a return of the compliment was necessary. Having always heard that Orientals turned menus topsy-turvy we were not at all surprised when the little serving women brought to each of us two silver plates and set them on our trays. These plates contained what appeared to be cake, one seeming to be angel food with icing, and the other fruit cake with the same covering. With these came bowls of soup, served in lacquer ware, made of glutinous nests of swallows, and also a salad made of shark fins. We ate the soup and salad and found it good, and then made tentative investigation of the "cake." To our great surprise we discovered the angel food to be fish and the "icing" was shredded and pressed lobster. The "fruit cake" developed into pressed dark meat of chicken, with an icing of pressed and glazed white meat of the same fowl.

Following this came the second service of tea, this time in cups of a rare yellow color and beautiful design, with similar teapot.

The next course was a mixture of immature vegetables, served in a sort of saute. These were sprouting beans, lentils, peas and a number of others with which we were unfamiliar. The whole was delicately flavored with a peculiar sauce.

After a short wait, during which the saki bottles circulated freely, one of the women came in bearing aloft a large silver tray on which reposed a mammoth crayfish, or California lobster. This appeared to be covered with shredded cocoanut, and when it was placed before the host for serving he was at loss, for no previous experience told him what to do. It developed that the shredded mass on top was the meat of the lobster which had been removed leaving the shell-fish in perfect form. It was served cold, with a peculiar sauce.

SAN FRANCISCO

Now followed the *piece de resistance*. A tub of water was brought in and in this was swimming a live fish, apparently of the carp family. After being on view for a few minutes it was removed and soon the handmaidens appeared with thinly sliced raw fish, served with soy sauce. Ordinarily one can imagine nothing more repulsive than a dish of raw fish, but we were tempted and did eat, and found it most delicious, delicate, and with a flavor of raw oysters.

Next came the third service of tea, this time in a deep red ware. Then came a dessert of unusual flavor and appearance, followed by preserved ginger and fruit.

It must be remembered that during the meal, which lasted from seven until past midnight, saki was served constantly yet no one felt its influence in more than a sense of increased exhilaration. It is customary to let the emptied bottles remain on the table until the close of the meal, and there was a mighty showing.

It was impossible to eat all that was set before us, but Japanese custom forbids such a breach of etiquette as an indication that the food was not perfection, consequently the serving maids appeared bearing six carved teak boxes, and placed one at each plate. Into these we arranged the food that was unconsumed, and when we went away we carried it with us. To cap the climax the Japanese stripped the room of its bounteous decoration of chrysanthemums and piled them into our arms and we went home loaded with food and flowers.

Proprietor and all his household accompanied us to the door with many bows and gesticulations, wishing us best of luck, and we went back to our homes in the desolated city with the feeling of having been transported to Fairyland of the Orient.

We discovered later that our Japanese friend was of the family of the Emperor and was here on a diplomatic mission.

BOHEMIAN

One cannot well write a book on Bohemian restaurants of San Francisco without saying something about the great hotel whose history is so intimately intertwined with that of the city since 1873, when William C. Ralston determined that the city by the Golden Gate should have a hotel commensurate with its importance. San Francisco and the Palace Hotel were almost synonymous all over the world, and it was conceded by travelers that nowhere else was there a hostelry to equal this great hotel.

OLD AND NEW PALACE

To the bon vivant the grills of the Palace Hotel contained more to enhance the joy of living than anywhere else, and here the chefs prided themselves with providing the best in the land, prepared in such perfect ways as to make a meal at the Palace the perfection of gastronomic art.

There are three distinct eras to the history of the Palace Hotel, the first being from 1876 to 1890, the second from 1890 to 1906, and the third from 1906 to the present day. In the earlier days the grills, both that for gentlemen and that for ladies, were noted for their magnificent service and their wonderful cooking. A breakfast in the Ladies' Grill, with an omelet of California oysters, toast and coffee, was a meal long to be remembered. Possibly the most famous dish of the old Palace was this one of omelet with California oysters, and it was prepared in the following manner:

OYSTER OMELET

(For two): Take six eggs, one hundred California oysters, one small onion, one tablespoonful of butter, one tablespoonful of flour, salt and pepper to taste. Beat the eggs to a froth and stir in the onion chopped fine. Put the eggs into an omelet pan over a slow fire. Mix the flour and butter to a soft paste with a little cream, and stir in with the oysters, adding salt and pepper to taste. When the eggs begin to stiffen pour the oysters over and turn the omelet together. Serve on hot plate with a dash of paprika.

SAN FRANCISCO

This is the recipe of Ernest Arbogast, the chef for many years of the old Palace. The slightly coppery taste of the California oysters gives a piquancy to the flavor of the omelet that can be obtained in no other way, and those who once ate of Arbogast's California oyster omelet, invariably called for it again and again.

OLD AND NEW PALACE

We asked Jules Dauviller, the present chef of the Palace, for the recipe of what he considered the best dish now prepared at the Palace and he said he would give us two, as it was difficult to decide which was the best and most distinctive. These are the recipes as he wrote them for us:

Trim some select fillet mignon of beef, about four ounces of each, nicely. Saute these in a frying pan with clarified butter on a hot fire. Dress on a small round plank, about four and a half inches in diameter, decorated with a border of mashed potatoes. Over the fillet mignon pour stuffed pimentoes, covered with a sauce made of fresh mushrooms, sauteed sec over which has been poured a little chateaubriand sauce. Serve chateaubriand sauce in a bowl.

PLANKED FILLET MIGNON

The second is:

Select six nice fresh sand-dabs. Raise the fillets from the bone, skin and pare nicely, and season with salt and paprika. Arrange them in an earthenware dish. Cut in Julienne one stalk of celery, one green pepper, one cucumber, two or three tomatoes, depending on their size.

COLD FILLET OF SAND-DABS, PALACE

With the bone of the sand-dab, well cleaned, make a stock with one bottle of Riesling, juice of one lemon and seasoning. Add chervil and tarragon. Season to taste and cook the Julienne ingredients with some of the stock. When the rest of the stock is boiling poach it in the fillets of sand-dab, then remove from the fire and let get cold. Put the garnishing around the fillets and put on ice to get in jelly. When ready to serve decorate around the dish with any kind of salad you like, and with beets, capers, olives and marinated mushrooms. This must be served very cold and you may serve mayonnaise sauce on the side.

BOHEMIAN

We asked Dauviller what he considered his most delicate salad and he gave us this recipe:

PALACE GRILL SALAD Select three hearts of celery and cut them Julienne. Cut some pineapple and pimentoes into dice. Mix all well together in a bowl and add mayonnaise sauce and a little whipped cream. Sprinkle some finely chopped green peppers on top and serve very cold.

SAN FRANCISCO

On the morning of April 18, 1906, one of us stood in the doorway of the Hotel St. Francis, and watched approaching fires that came from three directions. It was but a few hours later when all that part of the city was a mass of seething flames, and in the ruins that lay in the wake of devastation was this magnificent hostelry.

AT THE HOTEL ST. FRANCIS

Before business in the down-town district was reorganized, and while the work of removing the tangled masses of debris was still in progress the Merchants Association of San Francisco called its members together in its annual banquet, and this banquet was held in the basement of the Hotel St. Francis, the crumbling walls, and charred and blackened timbers hidden under a mass of bunting and foliage and flowers. Here was emphasized the spirit of Bohemian San Francisco, and it was one of the most merry and enjoyable of feasts ever held in the city.

It was made possible by the fact that the management of the Hotel St. Francis was undaunted in the face of almost overwhelming disaster. The same spirit has carried the hotel through stress of storm and it stands now, almost as a monument to the energy of James Woods, its manager. There has always been a soft spot in our hearts for the Hotel St. Francis, and it is here that we have always felt a most pleasurable emotion when seeking a place where good things are served. Whether it be in the magnificent white and gold dining room, or the old tapestry room that has been remodeled into a dining room, or in the electric grill below stairs, it has always been the same.

We asked Chef Victor Hertzler what he considered his best recipe and his answer was characteristic of him.

"I shall give you Sole Edward VII. If this is not satisfactory I can give you a meat, or a salad or a soup recipe." We considered it satisfactory, and here it is:

BOHEMIAN

SOLE EDWARD VII

Cut the fillets out of one sole and lay them flat on a buttered pan, and season with salt and pepper. Make the following mixture and spread over each fillet of sole: Take one-half pound of sweet butter, three ounces of chopped salted almonds, one-fourth pound of chopped fresh mushrooms, a little chopped parsley, the juice of a lemon, salt, pepper and a little grated nutmeg.

Add to the pan one-half glassful of white wine and put in the oven for twenty minutes.

When done serve in the pan by placing it on a platter, with a napkin under it.

Hertzler has another recipe which he prizes greatly and which he calls "Celery Victor," and this is the recipe which he gave us:

CELERY VICTOR

Take six stalks of celery well washed. Make a stock of one soup hen or chicken bones, and five pounds of veal bones in the usual manner, with carrots, onions, parsley, bay leaves, salt and pepper. Place the celery in a vessel and strain the broth over it. Boil until soft and let cool off in its own broth.

When cold press the broth out of the celery with the hand, gently, and place on a plate. Season with salt, fresh ground black pepper, chervil, and one-quarter white wine vinegar with tarragon to three-quarters of best olive oil.

SAN FRANCISCO

Streets centering around Powell from Market up to Geary, may well be termed the "Great White Way" of San Francisco, if New York will permit the plagiarism. Here are congregated the most noted of the lively restaurants of the present day San Francisco. Here the streets are ablaze with light at night, and thronged with people, for here is the restaurant and theatre district proper of the city.

AMID BRIGHT LIGHTS

Among the restaurants deserving of special mention in this district are the two Solaris. When Solari opened his restaurant at 354 Geary street, where he continues to attract good livers by the excellence of his cooking, he at once achieved fame which has never waned. It so happened that there were two brothers, and as sometimes occurs brothers disagreed with the result that Fred Solari withdrew and opened a restaurant at Geary and Mason, just a short distance from the original place.

Evidently the recipe for what is considered best in both of the Solari restaurants came from common ownership, for each of these places gave in response to a request for its best recipe, the following:

Cut a chicken in eight pieces and drop them into some cold milk, seasoning with salt. After soaking for a few minutes dry the chicken in flour and lay in a frying pan in good butter. Place in the oven and let them cook slowly, turning them occasionally until they are nice and brown on all sides, when remove them. In the gravy put a tumblerful of cream and a pinch of paprika, mix well and let it cook for ten minutes, until it gets thick, then strain and pour over the chicken and serve.

CHICKEN COUNTRY STYLE

The following "don'ts" are added to the recipe: Don't use frozen poultry. Don't substitute corn starch and milk for cream.

BOHEMIAN

San Francisco holds no more interesting district than that lying around the base of Telegraph Hill, and extending over toward North Beach, even as far as Fisherman's Wharf. Here is the part of San Francisco that first felt the restoration impulse, and this was the first part of San Francisco rebuilt after the great fire, and in its rebuilding it recovered all of its former characteristics, which is more than can be said of any other part of the rebuilt city.

AROUND LITTLE ITALY

Here, extending north from Jackson street to the Bay, are congregated Italians, French, Portuguese and Mexicans, each in a distinct colony, and each maintaining the life, manners and customs, and in some instances the costumes, of the parent countries, as fully as if they were in their native lands. Here are stores, markets, fish and vegetable stalls, bakeries, paste factories, sausage factories, cheese factories, wine presses, tortilla bakeries, hotels, pensions, and restaurants; each distinctive and full of foreign life and animation, and each breathing an atmosphere characteristic of the country from which the parent stock came.

Walk along the streets on the side of Telegraph Hill and one can well imagine himself transported to a sunny hillside in Italy, for here he hears no other language than that which came from the shores of the Mediterranean. Here are Italians of all ages, sexes and conditions of servitude, from the padrone to the bootblack who works for a pittance until he obtains enough to start himself in business. If one investigate closely it will be found that many of the people of this part of San Francisco have been here for years and still understand no other language than that of their native home. Why should they learn anything else, they say. Everybody around them, and with whom they come in contact speaks Italian. Here are the Corsicans, with their

SAN FRANCISCO

peculiar ideas of the vendetta and the cheapness of life in general, and the Sicilians and Genoese and Milanese. Here are some from the slopes of Vesuvius or Aetna, with inborn knowledge of the grape and of wine making. All have brought with them recipes and traditions, some dating back for

AROUND LITTLE ITALY

hundreds of years, or even thousands, to the days before the Christian Era was born. It is just the same to them as it was across the ocean, for they hear the same dialect and have the same customs. Do they desire any special delicacy from their home district, they need but go to the nearest Italian grocery store and get it, for these stores are supplied direct from Genoa or Naples. This is the reason that many of the older men and women still speak the soft dialect of their native communities, and if you are so unfortunate as not to be able to understand them, then it is you who are the loser.

Do you wish to know something about conditions in Mexico? Would you like to learn what the Mexicans themselves really think about affairs down in that disturbed republic? Go along Broadway west of Grant avenue, and then around the corner on Stockton, and you will see strange signs, and perhaps you will not know that "Fonda" means restaurant, or that "Tienda," means a store. But these are the signs you will see, and when you go inside you will hear nothing but the gentle Spanish of the Mexican, so toned down and so changed that some of the Castilians profess to be unable to understand it.

Here you will find all the articles of household use that are to be found in the heart of Mexico, and that have been used for hundreds of years despite the progress of civilization in other countries. You will find all the strange foods and all the inconsequentials that go to make the sum of Mexican happiness, and if you can get

BOHEMIAN

sufficiently close in acquaintance you will find that not only will they talk freely to you, but they will tell you things about Mexico that not even the heads of the departments in Washington are aware of.

AROUND LITTLE ITALY

Perhaps you would like to know something about the bourgeoise French, those who have come from the peasant district of the mother country. Go a little further up Broadway and you will begin to see the signs changing from Spanish to French, and if you can understand them you will know that here you will be given a dinner for twenty-five cents on week days and for thirty-five cents on Sundays. The difference is brought about by the difference between the price of cheap beef or mutton and the dearer chicken.

Up in the second story on a large building you may see a sign that tells you meals will be served and rooms provided. One of these is the rendezvous of Anarchists, who gather each evening and discuss the affairs of the world, and how to regulate them. But they are harmless Anarchists in San Francisco, for here they have no wrongs to redress, so they sit and drink their forbidden absinthe, and dream their dreams of fire and sword, while they talk in whispers of what they are going to do to the crowned heads of Europe. It is their dream and we have no quarrel with it or them.

But for real interest one must get back to the slope of Telegraph Hill; to the streets running up from Columbus avenue, until they are so steep that only goats and babies can play on them with safety. At least we suppose the babies are as active as the goats for the sides of the hill are alive with them.

Let us walk first along Grant avenue and do a little window shopping. Just before you turn off Broadway into Grant avenue, after passing the Fior d'Italia, the Buon Gusto, the Dante and Il Trovatore restaurants, we

SAN FRANCISCO

come to a most interesting window where is displayed such a variety of sausages as to make one wonder at the inventive genius who thought of them all. As you wonder you peep timidly in the door and then walk in from sheer amazement. You now find yourself surrounded with sausages, from floor to ceiling, and from side wall to side wall on both ceiling and floor, and such sausage it is!

AROUND LITTLE ITALY

From strings so thin as to appear about the size of a lady's little finger, to individual sausages as large as the thigh of a giant, they hang in festoons, crawl over beams, lie along shelves, decorate counters, peep from boxes on the floor, and invite you to taste them in the slices that lay on the butcher's block. One can well imagine being in a cave of flesh, yet if you look closely you will discover that sausage is but a part of the strange edible things to be had here.

Here are cheeses in wonderful variety. Cheeses from Italy that are made from goats' milk, asses' milk, cows' milk and mares' milk, and also cheeses from Spain, Mexico, Germany, Switzerland, and all the other countries where they make cheese, even including the United States. These cheeses are of all sizes and all shapes, from the great, round, flat cheese that we are accustomed to see in country grocery stores, to the queer-shaped caciocavallo, which looks like an Indian club and is eaten with fruit.

There are dried vegetables and dried fruits such as were never dreamed of in your limited experience, and even the grocer himself, the smiling and cosmopolitan Verga, confesses that he does not know the names of all of them.

As you go out into the street you blink at the transformation, for you have been thousands of miles away. You think that surely there can be nothing more. Wait a bit. Turn the corner and walk along Grant avenue

BOHEMIAN

AROUND LITTLE ITALY

toward the Hill. See, here is a window full of bread. Look closely at it and you will notice that it is not like the bread you are accustomed to. Count the different kinds. Fourteen of them in all, from the long sticks of grissini to the great solid loaves weighing many pounds. Light bread, heavy bread, good bread, soft bread, hard bread, delicate bread, each having its especial use, and all satisfying to different appetites.

Now go a little further to the corner, cross the street and enter the store of the Costa Brothers. It is a big grocery store and while you will not find the sausage and mystifying mass of food products in such lavish display and profuseness, as in the previous place, if you look around you will find this even more interesting, for it is on a different plane. Here you find the delicacies and the niceties of Italian living. At first glance it looks as if you were in any one of the American grocery stores of down-town, but a closer examination reveals the fact that these canned goods and these boxes and jars, hold peculiar foods that you are unaccustomed to. Perhaps you will find a clerk who can speak good English, but if you cannot either of the Costa brothers will be glad to show you the courtesy of answering your questions.

Turn around and look at the shelves filled with bottles of wine. Now you feel that you are on safe ground, for you know about wines and can talk about Cresta Blanca, and Mont Rouge, and Asti Colony Tipo Chianti. But wait a minute. Here are labels that you do not understand and wines that you never even heard of. Here are wines whose taste is so delicious that you wonder why it is the whole world is not talking about it and drinking it.

Here are wines from the slopes of Aetna, sparkling and sweet. Here are wines from grapes grown on the

SAN FRANCISCO

AROUND LITTLE ITALY

warm slopes of Vesuvius, and brought to early perfection by the underground fires. Here are wines from the colder slopes of mountains; wines from Parma and from Sicily and Palermo where the warm Italian sunshine has been the arch-chemist to bring perfection to the fruit of the vine.
Here are still wines and those that sparkle. Here the famed Lacrima Christi, both spumanti and fresco, said to be the finest wine made in all Italy, and the spumanti have the unusual quality for an Italian wine of being dry. But to tell you of all the interesting articles to be found in these Italian, and French and Mexican stores, would be impossible, for some of them have not been translated into English, and even the storekeepers would be at a loss for words to explain them.

This is all a part of the Bohemianism of San Francisco, and that is why we are telling you about it in a book that is supposed to be devoted to the Bohemian restaurants. The fact is that San Francisco's Bohemian restaurants would be far less interesting were it not for the fact that they can secure the delicacies imported by these foreign storekeepers to supply the wants of their people.

But do not think you have exhausted the wonders of Little Italy when you have left the stores, for there is still more to see. If you were ever in Palermo and went into the little side streets, you saw the strings of macaroni, spaghetti and other pastes drying in the sun while children and dogs played through and around it, giving you such a distaste for it that you have not eaten any Italian paste since.

But in San Francisco they do things differently. There are a number of paste factories, all good and all clean. Take that of P. Fiorini, for instance, at a point a short distance above Costa Brothers. You cannot miss

BOHEMIAN

it for it has a picture of Fiorini himself as a sign, and on it he tells you that if you eat his paste you will get to be as fat as he is. Go inside and you will find that Fiorini can talk just enough English to make himself understood, while his good wife, his sole assistant, can neither speak nor understand any but her native Italian. But that does not bother her in the least, for she can make signs, and you can understand them even better than you understand the English of her husband.

AROUND
LITTLE
ITALY

Here you will see the making of raviolis by the hundred at a time. Tagliarini, tortilini, macaroni, spaghetti, capellini, percatelli, tagliatelli, and all the seventy and two other varieties. The number of kinds of paste is most astonishing, and one wonders why there are so many kinds and what is done with them. Fiorini will tell you that each kind has its distinctive use. Some are for soups, some for sauces, and all for special edibility. There are hundreds of recipes for cooking the various pastes and each one is said to be a little better than the others, if you can imagine such a thing.

Turn another corner after leaving Fiorini's and look down into a basement. You do not have to go to the country to see wine making. Here is one of the primitive wine presses of Italy, and if you want to know why some irreverent people call the red wine of the Italians "Chateau la Feet," you have but to watch the process of its making in these Telegraph Hill wine houses. The grapes are poured into a big tub and a burly man takes off his shoes and socks and emulates the oxen of Biblical times when it treaded out the grain. Of course he washes his feet before he gets into the wine tub. But, at that, it is not a pleasant thing to contemplate. Now you look around with wider and more comprehensive eyes, and now you begin to under-

SAN FRANCISCO

AROUND LITTLE ITALY

stand something about these strange foreign quarters in San Francisco. As you look around you note another thing. Italian fecundity is apparent everywhere, and the farther up the steep slope of the Hill you go the more children you see. They are everywhere, and of all sizes and ages, in such reckless profusion that you no longer wonder if the world is to be depopulated through the coming of the fad of Eugenics. The Italian mother has but two thoughts—her God and her children, and it is to care for her children that she has brought from her native land the knowledge of cookery, and of those things that help to put life and strength in their bodies.

An Italian girl said to us one day:

"Mama knows nothing but cooking and going to church. She cooks from daylight until dark, and stops cooking only when she is at church."

It was evident that her domestic and religious duties dominated her life, and she knew but two things—to please her God and to care for her family, and without question if occasion demanded the pleasure of her family took precedence.

San Francisco's Latin quarter is appealing, enticing and hypnotizing. Go there and you will learn why San Francisco is a Bohemian city. You will find out that so many things you have thought important are really not at all worth while. Go there and you will find the root of Bohemian restaurants. These people have studied gastronomy as a science, and they have imparted their knowledge to San Francisco, with the result that the Bohemian spirit enters into our very lives, and our minds are broadened, and our views of life and our ideas have a wider scope. It is because of this condition, born on the slopes of Telegraph Hill, that we are drawn out of depressing influences, out of the spirit of self-consciousness, and find a world of pleasure, innocent and educa-

BOHEMIAN

AROUND LITTLE ITALY

tional, the inspiration for which has been handed down through generations of Latins since the days of early Roman empire, which inspiration is still a power for good because it takes people out of themselves and places them where they can look with understanding and speak the language of perception. Little Italy's charm has long been recognized by artists and writers, and many of them began their careers which led to fame and fortune in little cheap rooms on Telegraph Hill. Here have lived many whose names are now known to fame, and to name them would be almost like a directory of world renowned artists and writers. Here is still the memory of Bret Harte and Mark Twain. Here is where Keith had his early studio. Cadenasso, Martinez, and many others know these slopes and love them.

To all these and many more the Latin Quarter of San Francisco possessed a charm they could find nowhere else, and if one desire to bring a saddened look to the faces of many now living elsewhere it is but necessary to talk of the good old days when Bohemia was on Telegraph Hill in San Francisco. Here they had their domicile, and here they foregathered in the little restaurants, whose claims to merit lay chiefly in the fact that they were rarely visited by other than the Italians of the quarter and these Bohemians who lived there.

Here was the inspiration of many a good book and many a famous picture whose inception came from thoughts that crystallized amid these surroundings, and here many a needy Bohemian struggled through the lean days with the help of these kind-hearted Latins. Here they, even as we, were taught something of the art of cooking.

Of course, if one desire to learn various methods of preparing food, it is necessary to keep both eyes open

SAN FRANCISCO

and to ask many questions, seeking the information that sometimes comes from unlooked for sources. Even at that it is not always a good idea to take everything for granted or to accept every suggestion, for you may meet with the Italian vegetable dealer who is so eager to please his customers that he pretends a knowledge he does not possess. We discovered him one day when he had on display a vegetable that was strange to us.

AROUND LITTLE ITALY

"How do you cook it?" was our question.

"Fry it."

Then his partner shouted his laughter and derision.

"Oh, he's one fine cook. All the time he say 'fry it.' One day a lady she come into da store an' she see da big bucket of ripe olives. Da lady she from the East and she never see olives like dat before. 'How you cook it?' say da lady. 'Fry it,' say my partner. Everything he say fry it."

In another vegetable stand we found an Italian girl, whose soft lisping accent pronounced her a Genoese, and she diffidently suggested "a fine Italian dessert."

"You take macaroons and strawberries. Put a layer of macaroons in a dish and then a layer of strawberries, cover these with sugar, and then another layer of macaroons and strawberries and sugar until you have all you want. Over these pour some rum and set fire to it. After it is burned out you have a fine dessert."

A FINE DESSERT

We bought the macaroons and strawberries on the way home and did not even wait for dinner time to try it. We pronounce it good.

It was made the right way and we advise you to try it, for it is simple and leaves a most delicious memory.

BOHEMIAN

It was very early one morning. So early that one of us strenuously pretended sleep while the other gave urgent reminder that this was the day we were to go to Fishermen's Wharf. Daylight came early and it was just four o'clock when we began preparations. A cup of hot coffee while dressing served to get us wide-awake, and we were off to see the fish come in.

WHERE
FISH
COME IN

Fishermen's Wharf lies over at North Beach, at the end of Meiggs's Wharf, where the Customs Officers have their station, and to reach it one takes either the Powell and North Beach cars, or the Kearny and North Beach cars, and at the end of either walks two blocks. When you get that far anybody you see can tell you where to go.

Fog mist was stealing along the Marin shore, and hiding Golden Gate when we arrived, and the rays of the sun took some time to make a clear path out to sea. Out of the bank of white came gliding the heavy power boats of the Sicilian and Corsican fishermen, while from off shore were the ghostly lateen rigged boats of those who had been fishing up the Sacramento and San Joaquin rivers, their yards aslant to catch the faint morning breeze. As they slipped through the leaden water to their mooring at the wharf we could see the decks and holds piled with fish and crabs.

Roosting on piles, and lining the water's edge on everything that served to give foothold, were countless seagulls, all waiting for the breakfast they knew was coming from the discarded fish, and fit companions were the women with shawls over their heads irreverently called mud hens, and old men in dilapidated clothing, who sat along the stringers of the wharf, some with baskets, some with buckets and others with little paper bags, in which to put the fish which they could get so cheaply it meant a meal for them when other-

SAN FRANCISCO

wise they would have to go without. The earlier boats were moored and on the decks fires were burning in charcoal braziers, on which the fishermen cooked their breakfasts of fish and coffee, with the heavy black loaves of bread for which they seem to have special fancy. As the odor of the cooking fish came up from the water the waiting gulls and men and women moved a little closer.

WHERE FISH COME IN

Breakfast over the fishermen turned to the expectant crowd and began taking notice of the pitiful offerings of coin. Tin buckets, newspapers, bags, rags and even scooped hands were held down, each containing such coin as the owner possessed, and in return came bountiful supply of fish. A fine, fat crab for which your market man would charge you forty cents was sold for ten. Beautiful, fresh sand-dabs, but an hour or two out of the water, were five cents a pound, while sea bass, fresh cod, mackerel, and similar fish went at the same price. Small fish, or white bait, went by quantity, ten cents securing about half a gallon. Smelt, herring, flounder, sole, all went at equally low prices, and as each buyer secured his allotment he went hurrying off through the mist, as silently as the floating gulls. When these were all supplied the rest of the fish and crabs were taken up to the wharf and put on the counters of the free market, where they were sold at prices most tempting.

Shrimps, alive and active, crayfish, clams, squid and similar sea food was in profusion and sold at prices on a parity with that of the fish. As the day wore on the early buyers were replaced by those who knew of the free fish market and came to get good supplies for their money. Here were boarding-house keepers, unmistakable anywhere, Bohemians in hard luck who remembered that they could get good food here at a minimum of price, and came now while on the down turn of the wheel.

BOHEMIAN

As a human interest study it was better than a study of fish. Fishermen's Wharf is where the independent fishermen bring their catches to San Francisco, but it is not where the city's great supply comes in. To see that we had to go along the docks until we came to the Broadway wharf where Paladini, the head of the fish trust, unloads his tugs of their tons and tons of fish. It is not nearly so interesting to look at, but it gives a good idea of what comes out of the sea every day to supply the needs of San Francisco and the surrounding country. These tugs bring in the catches of dozens of smaller boats manned by fishermen who are toiling out beyond the heads, and up the two great rivers. From far out around the Farallones, from up around the Potato Patch with its mournful fog bell constantly tolling, from down the coast as far as Monterey Bay where fish are in such abundance that it is said they have to give a signal when they want to turn around, from up the rivers, come fish to the man who has grown from the owner of a small sail boat to be the power who controls prices of all the fish that go to the markets of the city.

WHERE FISH COME IN

By the time we finished with Paladini's fish we felt ready for breakfast and took a car down to Davis and Pacific street where we found Bazzuro's serving breakfast to dozens of market gardeners who had finished their unloading, and there, while partaking of the fresh fish we had brought from Fishermen's Wharf, we saw another phase of San Francisco's early morning life. Here were gardeners who came in the darkness of early morning to supply hucksters, small traders and a few thrifty people who knew of the cheapness, and in Columbo market they drove their great wagons and discharged their day's gathering of vegetables of all kinds.

But a few steps away is the great fruit market of the early morning and here tons of the finest fruits are dis-

SAN FRANCISCO

tributed to the hundreds of wagons that crowd the street to such an extent that it takes all the ingenuity of experienced policemen to keep clearway for traffic. Threading their way in and out between the wheels and the heels of horses, were men and women, all looking for bargains in food. Amid a din almost deafening business was transacted with such celerity that in three hours the streets were cleared, fruits and vegetables sold and on their way to distant stands, and the tired policemen leaning gainst friendly walls, recuperating after the strenuous work of keeping order in chaos.

WHERE FISH COME IN

It is when one goes to these places in the morning and sees the cheapness of these foods that he can understand in a small way why it is that so many Italian restaurants can give such good meals for so little money. One wonders at a table d'hote dinner of six or seven courses for twenty-five cents, or even for half a dollar, and one accustomed to buying meats, fish, vegetables and fruits at the exorbitant prices charged at most of the markets and fruit and vegetable stands now sees why the thrifty foreigner can make and save money while the average American can hardly keep more than two jumps ahead of the sheriff.

BOHEMIAN

Probably the most frequent question asked us by those who come to San Francisco is: "Where can we get the best fish?" With San Francisco's wonderful natural advantages as a fish market one is sometimes surprised that more attention is not given to preparing fish as a specialty. But one restaurant in the city deals exclusively with sea food, and even there one is astonished at an overlooked opportunity.

FISH IN THEIR VARIETY

Darbee & Immel have catered to San Francisco in oysters for many years and after the fire they opened the Shell Fish Grotto, in O'Farrell street, between Powell and Mason streets, and this is one of the very few distinctive fish restaurants of the country. It is when one considers the possibilities that a shock comes from the environing decorations. White and gold pillars, with twining ivy reaching to the old gold and rose mural and ceiling embellishments seem out of place in a restaurant that is devoted entirely to catering to lovers of fish. Nothing in the place indicates its character except the big lobster in front of the building. Not even so much as a picture to bring a sentiment of the ocean to the mind.

We are going to take a liberty, and possibly Darbee & Immel may call it an impertinence, and give them a bit of advice. It costs them nothing consequently they can act on it or not and it will make no difference. This is our suggestion:

Change the interior of the place entirely by having around the walls a series of large glass aquaria, with as many different kinds of fish swimming about as it is possible to get; something on the order of the interior of the aquarium in Battery Park in New York. Paint the ceiling to represent the surface of the water as seen from below. Have seaweed and kelp in place of ivy, and a fish net or two caught up in the corners of the

SAN FRANCISCO

room, with here and there a star fish or a crab—not too many, for profuseness in this sort of decoration is an abomination. Then you will have a restaurant that will be talked about wherever people sit at meat. But to get back to our talk about fish, and where to get it prepared and cooked the best. *FISH IN THEIR VARIETY* We must say that the finest fish we have eaten in San Francisco was not in the high-priced restaurants at all, but in a little, dingy back room, down at Fishermen's Wharf, where there was sand on the floor and all the sounds of the kitchen were audible in the dining room. The place was patronized almost solely by the Italian fishermen who not only know how to catch a fish but how it ought to be cooked. One may always rest assured that when he gets a fish in one of the Italian restaurants it is perfectly fresh, for there are two things that an Italian demands in eating, and they are fresh fish and fresh vegetables.

At the Gianduja at Union and Stockton streets, one is certain to get fish cooked well and that it is perfectly fresh. The variety is not so good as at the Shell Fish Grotto, but otherwise it is just as good in every respect. At the Grotto there is a wonderful variety but the quantity is at the minimum because there, too, they will have no fish that has been twenty-four hours out of the water.

One wonders how a full course dinner entirely of fish can be prepared, but if you will go to the Shell Fish Grotto you will find that it is done, and done well at that. Here you can get a good dinner for one dollar, or if you prefer it they have a Fish Dinner de Luxe for which they charge two dollars. Both are good, the latter having additional wines and delicacies.

Down in Washington street, just off Columbus avenue, is the Vesuvius, an Italian restaurant of low price, but excellent cooking. A specialty there is fish which

BOHEMIAN

is always brought fresh from the nearby Clay street market as ordered, consequently is perfect. When you give your order a messenger is dispatched to the market and usually he brings the fish alive and the chef prepares it in one of his many ways, for he is said to have more secrets about the cooking of fish than one would think it possible for one brain to contain. The trouble about this restaurant is that the rest of the menu does not come up to the fish standard, but if you desire a simple luncheon of fish there is no better place to get it.

FISH IN THEIR VARIETY

There are three things in which an Easterner will be disappointed in San Francisco, and these are oysters. Pacific Coast oysters fail in size, flavor and cooking, when compared with the luscious bivalve of the Atlantic, so far as the ordinary forms of preparation is concerned. Even fancy dishes, such as Oysters Kirkpatrick, would be better if made of the eastern oyster, not what they call the eastern oyster here, for that is a misnomer, but the oysters that grow in the Atlantic Ocean.

Of the Pacific oysters the best is the Toke Point, that comes from Oregon. They are similar in size to the Blue Point, but lack the flavor. When, in a San Francisco restaurant, you are asked what sort of oyster you will have, and you see the familiar names on the menu card, remember that these are transplanted oysters, and have lost much of their flavor in the transplanting, or else they are oysters that have been shipped across the continent and have thereby lost their freshness.

The California oyster proper, is very small, and it has a peculiar coppery taste, which bon vivants declare adds to its piquancy. Instead of ordering these by the dozen you order them by the hundred, it being no difficult task to eat an hundred at a meal, especially when prepared in a pepper roast.

SAN FRANCISCO

Everyone knows the staple ways of preparing oysters, and every chef looks upon the oyster as the source of new flavors in many dishes, but to our mind the best way we have found in San Francisco was at a little restaurant down in Washington street before the fire. It was the Buon Gusto. *FISH IN THEIR VARIETY* where they served fish and oysters better than anything else because the owners were the chefs, and they were from the island of Catalan, off the coast of Italy. Their specialty was called "Oysters a la Catalan," and their recipe, which is given, can be prepared excellently in a chafing dish:

Take one tablespoonful of butter, two teaspoonfuls grated Edam or Parmesan cheese, four tablespoonfuls catsup, one- *OYSTERS A LA CATALAN* half teaspoonful Worcestershire sauce, two tablespoonfuls cream, meat of one good-sized crab cut fine and two dozen oysters. Put the cheese and butter into a double boiler and when melted smooth add the catsup and Worcestershire sauce. Mix well and add the cream and then the crab meat. When creamy and boiling hot drop in the oysters. As soon as the oysters are crinkled serve on hot buttered toast on hot plates.

In the days before the fire when you went to a restaurant and ordered fish or oysters the waiter invariably put before you either a plate of crab salad or a dish of shrimps, with which you were supposed to amuse yourself while the meal was being prepared. Shrimps and crabs were then so plentiful that their price was never considered. Under our new conditions these always appear on the bill when ordered, and if they be not ordered they do not appear for they now are made to increase the income.

To the uninitated visitor the shrimps so served were always something of a mystery, and after a few futile efforts to get at the meat they generally gave it up as too much work for the little good derived. The Old Timer, however, cracked the shrimp's neck, pinched its tail,

BOHEMIAN

and out popped a delicious bonne bouche which added to the joy of the meal and increased the appetite. But there are many other ways of serving shrimps, and they are also much used to give flavor to certain fish sauces. One of the most delicious ways of preparing shrimp is what is known as "Shrimp Creole, a la Antoine," so named after the famous New Orleans Antoine by a chef in San Francisco who had regard for the New Orleans caterer. We doubt if it can be had anywhere in San Francisco now unless you are well enough known to have it prepared according to the recipe. This recipe, by the way, is a good one to use in a chafing dish supper. This is the way it was prepared at the old Pup restaurant, one of the noted restaurants before the fire and earthquake changed conditions:

FISH IN THEIR VARIETY

SHRIMP CREOLE

Take three pints of unshelled shrimps and shell them, one-half pint of cream, two tablespoonfuls of butter, two tablespoonfuls of flour, two tablespoonfuls of catsup, one wine glass of sherry, paprika, chili powder and parsley. Brown the flour in the butter and add the milk until it is thickened. Color with the catsup and season with paprika and chili powder. Stir in the sherry and make a pink cream which is to be mixed through the shrimps and not cooked. Sprinkle with chopped parsley and serve with squares of toast or crackers.

SAN FRANCISCO

When is a lobster not a lobster? When it is a crayfish. This question and answer might well go into the primer of information for those who come to San Francisco from the East, for what is called a lobster in San Francisco is not a lobster at all but a crayfish. The true lobster is not found in the Pacific along the California coast, and so far efforts at transplanting have not been successful. The Pacific crayfish, however, serves every purpose, and while many contend that its meat is not so delicate in flavor as that of its eastern cousin, the Californian will as strenuously insist that it is better, but, of course, something must always be allowed for the patriotism of the Californian.

LOBSTERS
AND
LOBSTERS

Lobster, served cold with mayonnaise, or broiled live lobster are most frequently called for, and while they are both excellent, we find so many other ways of preparing this crustacean that we rarely take the common variety of lobster dishes into consideration. Probably nowhere in San Francisco could one get lobster better served than in the Old Delmonico restaurant of the days before the fire. A book could be written about this restaurant and then all would not be told for all its secrets can never be known.

In New York City they have what they are pleased to call "Lobster Palaces," but there is not a restaurant in that great metropolis that could approach the Delmonico of San Francisco in its splendid service and its cuisine arrangements; neither could they approach the romance that always surrounded the O'Farrell street restaurant. It was here that most magnificent dinners were arranged; it was here that extraordinary dishes were concocted by chefs of world-wide fame; it was here that Lobster a la Newberg reached its highest perfection, and this is the recipe that was followed when it was prepared in the Delmonico:

BOHEMIAN

LOBSTER A LA NEWBERG

One pound of lobster meat, one teaspoonful of butter, one-half pint of cream, yolks of four eggs, one wine glass of sherry, lobster fat. Three hours before cooking pour the sherry over the lobster meat and let it stand until ready to cook. Heat the butter and stir in with the lobster and wine, then place this in a stewpan, or chafing dish, and cook for eight minutes. Have the yolks of eggs well beaten and add to them the cream and lobster fat, stir well and then stir in a teaspoonful of flour. Put this in a double boiler and let cook until thick, stirring constantly. When this is cooked pour it over the lobster and let all cook together for three minutes. Serve in a chafing dish with thin slices of dry toast.

SAN FRANCISCO

One has to come to San Francisco to partake of the king of shell fish—the mammoth Pacific crab. I say "come to San Francisco" advisedly, for while the crab is found all along the coast it is prepared nowhere so deliciously as in San Francisco. Of course our friends in Portland will take exception to this, but the fact remains that nowhere except in San Francisco have so many restaurants become famous because of the way they prepare the crab. The Pacific crab is peculiar, and while it has not the gigantic claws such as are to be seen on those in the Parisian and London markets, its meat is much more delicate in flavor, and the dishes of crab prepared by artists of the gastronomic profession in San Francisco are more savory than those found elsewhere.

KING OF SHELL FISH

In the pre-fire days there were many places which paid especial attention to the cooking of the crab, among them being the Cobweb Palace, previously mentioned, and Gobey's. Gobey ran one of those places which was not in good repute, consequently when ladies went there they were usually veiled and slipped in through an alley, but the enticement of Gobey's crab stew was too much for conventionality and his little private rooms were always full.

Gobey's passed with the fire, and the little restaurant bearing his name, and in charge of his widow, in Union Square avenue, has not attained the fame of the old place. It is possible that she knows the secret of preparing crab as it was prepared in the Gobey's of before the fire, but his prestige did not descend to her.

Almost all of the Italian restaurants will give you crab in many forms, and all of them are good; many restaurants use crab meat for flavoring other dishes, but of all the recipes for cooking crab we have found none that we consider so good as that of Gobey's. It is as follows:

BOHEMIAN

GOBEY'S CRAB STEW

Take the meat of one large crab, scraping out all of the fat from the shell. One good-sized onion, one tomato, one sweet pepper, one teaspoonful of butter, one teaspoonful of flour, half a glass of sherry, a pinch of rosemary, one clove of garlic, paprika, salt and minionette pepper. Soak the crab meat in the sherry two hours before cooking. Chop fine the onion, sweet pepper and tomato with the rosemary. Mash the clove of garlic, rubbing thoroughly in a mortar and on this put the butter and flour, mixing well together, and gradually adding the salt and minionette pepper, and stir in two tablespoonfuls of cream. Heat this in a stewpan and when simmering add the sherry and crab meat and let all cook together with a slow fire for eight minutes. serve in a chafing dish with toasted crackers or thin slices of toasted bread. A dash of Worcestershire sauce just before it is taken up adds to the flavor.

SAN FRANCISCO

Crawfish, or ecravisse, has never been very popular in San Francisco, probably because there are so many other delicate crustaceans that are more easily handled, yet the crawfish grows to perfection in Pacific waters, and importations of them from Portland, Oregon, are becoming quite an industry. So far it has been used mostly for garnishment of other dishes, and it is only recently that the Hof Brau has been making a specialty of them. All of the better class restaurants, however, will serve them if you order them.

LOBSTER IN MINIATURE

The full flavor of the crawfish is best obtained in a bisque, and the best recipe for this is by the famous chef Francatelli, who boasts having been the head of the cuisine of Queen Victoria. His recipe is long, and its preparation requires much patience, but the result is such a gastronomic marvel that one never regrets the time spent in its accomplishment. This is the recipe for eight people, and it is well worth trying if you are giving a dinner of importance:

Take thirty crawfish, from which remove the gut containing the gall in the following manner: Take firm hold of the crawfish with the left hand so as to avoid being pinched by its claws; with the thumb and forefinger of the right hand pinch the extreme end of the central fin of the tail, and, with a sudden jerk, the gut will be withdrawn.

BISQUE OF CRAWFISH

Mince or cut into small dice a carrot, an onion, one head of celery and a few parsley roots, and to these add a bay leaf, a sprig of thyme, a little minionette pepper and two ounces of butter. Put these ingredients into a stewpan and fry them ten minutes, then throw in the crawfish and pour on them half a bottle of French white wine. Allow this to boil and then add a quart of strong consomme and let all continue boiling for half an hour. Pick out the crawfish and strain the broth through a napkin by pressure into a basin in order to extract all the essence from the vegetables.

Pick the shells off twenty-five of the crawfish tails, trim them neatly and set them aside until wanted. Reserve some of

BOHEMIAN

BISQUE OF CRAWFISH

the spawn, also half of the body shells with which to make the crawfish butter to finish the soup. This butter is made as follows: Place the shells on a baking sheet in the oven to dry; let the shells cool and then pound them in a mortar with a little lobster coral and four ounces of fresh butter, thoroughly bruising the whole together so as to make a fine paste. Put this in a stewpan and set it over a slow fire to simmer for about five minutes, then rub it through a sieve with considerable pressure into a basin containing ice water. As soon as the colored crawfish butter is become firmly set, through the coldness of the water, take it out and put it into a small basin and set in the refrigerator until wanted.

Reverting to the original recipe: Take the remainder of the crawfish and add thereto three anchovies, washed for the purpose, and also the crusts of French rolls, fried to a light brown color in butter. Pound all these thoroughly together and then put them into a stewpan with the broth that has been reserved in a basin, and having warmed the bisque thus prepared rub it through a sieve into a fine puree. Put this puree into a soup pot and finish by incorporating therewith the crawfish butter and season with a little cayenne pepper and the juice of half a lemon. Pour the bisque quite hot into the tureen in which have been placed the crawfish tails, and send to the table.

This is not so difficult as it appears when you are reading it and if you wish to have something extra fine take the necessary time and patience and prepare it.

SAN FRANCISCO

We cannot dispose of the shell fish of San Francisco without a word or two about clams, for certainly there is no place where they are in greater variety and better flavor. In fact the clam is the only bivalve of this part of the coast that has a distinctive and good flavor. Several varieties are to be found in the markets, the best and rarest being the little rock clams that come from around Drake's Bay, just above the entrance to Golden Gate. These are most delicious in flavor and should never be eaten otherwise than raw. The sand, or hard shell, or as they are sometimes called little necks, are next in choiceness, and then come the Pismo beach clams, noted for their flavor and enormous size. The mud clam is good for chowder but not so good as either of the other varieties mentioned.

CLAMS AND ABALONES

The Bohemian way to have your clams is to go to the shore of Bolinas Bay or some other equally retired spot, and have a clam bake, or else take a pot along with the other ingredients and have a good clam chowder. This, however, may be prepared at any time and is always a good meal.

Clam fritters when prepared according to the recipe given herein, is one of the best methods of preparing the clam, and it has the peculiarity of being so tasty that one feels that there is never enough cooked.

Of all the ways of cooking clams chowder takes precedence as a rule, and it is good when made properly. By that we do not mean the thin, watery stuff that is served in most of the restaurants and called clam chowder just because it happens to be made every Friday. That is fairly good as a clam soup but it is no more chowder than a Mexican soup approaches a crawfish bisque. There is but one right way to make clam chowder, and that is either to make it yourself or closely superintend the making, and this is the way to make it:

BOHEMIAN

CLAM CHOWDER

Take one quart of shelled sand clams, two large potatoes, two large onions, one clove of garlic, one sweet pepper, one thick slice of salt pork, one-half pound small oyster crackers, one-half glass sherry, one tablespoonful Worcestershire sauce, one tomato, salt, and pepper. In a large stewpan place the salt pork cut into small dice, and let this fry slightly over a slow fire until the bottom of the stewpan is well greased. Take this off the fire and put in a layer of potatoes sliced thin, on top of the salt pork, then a layer of onions sliced thin, and a layer of clams. Put on this salt and pepper and sprinkle with a little flour and then a layer of crackers. Chop the sweet pepper and tomato fine and mix with them the bruised and mashed garlic. On top of each succession of layers put a little of the mixture. Continue making these layers until all the ingredients are placed in the stewpan, and then pour on the top sufficient water to just show. Cover tightly and let cook gently for half an hour. Pour on the Worcestershire sauce and sherry just before serving. Do not stir this while cooking, and in order to prevent its burning it should be cooked over an asbestos cover.

When done this should be thick enough to be eaten with a fork.

Among the good Bohemians who lived in San Francisco as a child when it was in the post-pioneer days, and who has enjoyed the good things of all the famous restaurants is Mrs. Emma Sterett, who has given us the following recipe for clam fritters which we consider the most delicious of all we have ever eaten, and when you try them you will agree with us:

CLAM FRITTERS

Take two dozen clams, washed thoroughly and drained. Put in chopping bowl and chop, not too fine. Add to these one clove of garlic mashed, one medium-sized onion chopped fine, add bread crumbs sufficient to stiffen the mass, chopped parsley, celery and herbs to taste. Beat two eggs separately and add to the clams. If too stiff to drop from a spoon add the strained liquor of clams. Drop tablespoonfuls of this mixture into hot fat, turn and cook for sufficient time to cook through, then drain on brown paper and serve.

Abalones are a univalve that has been much in vogue among the Chinese but has seldom found place

SAN FRANCISCO

on the tables of restaurants owing to the difficulty in preparing them, as they are tough and insipid under ordinary circumstances. When made tender either by the Chinese method of pounding, or by steeping in vinegar, they serve the purpose of clams but have not the fine flavor. The Hof Brau restaurant is now making a specialty of abalones, but it takes sentiment to say that one really finds anything extra good in them.

CLAMS AND ABALONES

Another shell fish much in vogue among the Italian restaurants is mussels, which are found to perfection along the coast. These are usually served Bordelaise, and make quite a pleasant change when one is surfeited with other shell fish, but the best recipe is:

Thoroughly clean the mussels and then put them in a deep pan and pour over them half a glass of white wine. Chop an onion, a clove of garlic and some parsley fine and put in the pan, together with a tablespoonful of butter. Let these boil very quick for twelve minutes, keeping the pan tightly covered. Take off half shells and place the mussels in a chafing dish and pour over them Bechamel sauce and then add sufficient milk gravy to cover. Serve hot from chafing dish.

MUSSELS MARINIERE

BOHEMIAN

According to David Starr Jordan, acknowledged world authority on fish, there is greater variety of fish in Monterey Bay than anywhere else in the world. Monterey Bay is one of San Francisco's sources of supply consequently we have a greater variety of fish in our markets than are to be found anywhere else. In the markets are fish from all parts of the Pacific Ocean, from the Tropics to far north in the Arctics, while denizens of the waters all the way between add to the variety.

WHERE
FISH
ABOUND

The essential element of goodness in fish is freshness, and it is always fresh in San Francisco markets, and also in the restaurants. Of all varieties two rank first in the estimation of gourmets, but, of course, that is purely a matter of individual taste. According to the above-mentioned authority, "the finest fish that swims is the sand-dab." Some gourmets, however, will take issue with him on this and say the pompano is better. Others will prefer the mountain trout. Be that as it may they all are good, with many others following close in choice.

Fine striped bass from the ocean, or black bass from the fresh water takes high place in preference. Then there is sole, both in the fillet and Rex, as prepared at Jule's under the Monadnock building. Tom cod, rock cod, fresh mackerel and fresh cod, white bait and boned smelt all are excellent fish, but were we to attempt to tell of all the fish to be found here we would have to reproduce a piscatorial directory. There are two good methods of acquiring knowledge of the fish of San Francisco. Go to the wharves and see them come and and go to the wholesale markets down in Clay street, below Montgomery. You will then begin to realize that we certainly do have a variety of good fish.

Now for a little Bohemianism of a different sort: Recently there came to San Francisco, with his wife, an

SAN FRANCISCO

actor whose name used to be almost a household word among theater-goers, and when we say "the villain still pursued her," all you oldtimers will know whom we mean. When he was here in the years long gone by it was his custom to go to the old California market, select what he desired to eat, then take it to the restaurant and have it cooked, and the old atmosphere came back to him on his recent arrival and he revived the old custom.

WHERE FISH ABOUND

"Meet us at the California market," was the telephone message that came to us, and we were there, for we knew that something good was in store for us.

First we went through the market from end to end and all the side aisles, "spying out the land." It is not possible to enumerate what we saw. If you want to know go there and see for yourselves. Having seen we were told to go and select what we wished to have for our dinner, and then the selection began and there was a feast of buying fish, meats, vegetables and delicacies of all sorts, even to French pastry.

Our purchases were ordered sent to the restaurant in the corner of the market where the chef had already been duly "seen," and then came each particular idea as to how the food was to be cooked. We had sand-dabs munier, chateaubriand with mushrooms, Italian squash, fried in oil with a flavor of garlic, French pastry, and coffee, together with some good California Tipo Chianti, all flavored with such a stream of reminiscence that we forgot that such things as clocks existed.

It was the first time our theatrical friends had tasted sand-dabs, for this fish has come to San Francisco markets only in recent years, and they declared that it was the "only" fish fit to be eaten. It is possible that they were prejudiced by the sentiment of the surroundings and consequently not exactly in position to be good judges.

BOHEMIAN

All Italian restaurants serve fish well. At the New Buon Gusto you will find a most excellent cippino with polenti, and if you have not experienced this we advise you to try it as soon as possible. At the Gianduja you will find sand-dabs au gratin to be very fine. At Jack's, striped bass cooked in wine is what we think the best of the fish to be found in the market, or at the restaurants, cooked that way. Jule's is famous for his Rex sole. At all of the French and Italian restaurants small fry is cooked to perfection. If you wish fish in any way or of any kind you will make no mistake in asking for it at any of the French or Italian restaurants, or at the Shell Fish Grotto, and if you are in doubt regarding what to order just take the proprietor into your confidence, tell him you are a stranger in the city and ask him to serve you fish the best way he prepares it. You will not be disappointed.

WHERE FISH ABOUND

SAN FRANCISCO

Variants of food preparation sometimes typify nationalities better even than variants of language or clothing. Take the lowly corn meal, for instance. We find that Italian polenti, Spanish tamale, Philadelphia scrapple and Southern Darkey crackling corn bread are but variants of the preparation of corn meal in delectable foods. **SOME FOOD VARIANTS** It is a long step from plain corn meal mush to scrapple, which we consider the highest and best form of preparing this sort of dish, but all the intermediate steps come from a desire to please the taste with a change from simple corn meal. Crackling corn bread is the first step, and here we find that the darkies of the South found good use for the remnants of the pork after lard was tried out at hog-killing time, by mixing the cracklings with their corn meal and making a pone which they cooked before an open fire on a hoe blade, the first of this being called "cracklin' hoe cake."

Good scrapple is one of the finest breakfast dishes that we know during the winter, and when prepared after the recipe given here it precedes all other forms of serving corn meal. To mix it properly one must know the proper values of herbs and condiments, and this recipe is the result of much discriminating study. Modesty prevents us giving it more than the name of "scrapple." It is prepared in the following manner, differing from that made in Philadelphia:

Take a young pig's head and boil it until the flesh drops from the bones, in water **SCRAPPLE** to which has been added two good-sized onions, quartered, five bruised cloves of garlic, one bay leaf, sweet marjoram, thyme, rosemary, a little sage, salt, and pepper. Separate the meat from the bones and chop fine. Strain off the liquor and boil with corn meal, adding the chopped meat. Put in the corn meal gradually, until it makes a stiff mush, then cook for half an hour with the meat. Put in shallow pans and let cool. To serve slice about half an inch thick and fry in olive oil or butter to a light brown.

BOHEMIAN

As originally prepared the tamale was made for conveyance, hence the wrappings of corn husk. This is a Spanish dish, having been brought to this country by the early Spanish explorers, and adopted by the Indian tribes with whom they came in contact. In the genuine tamale the interior is the sauce and meat that goes with the corn meal which is alternately laid with the husks, and when made the ends are tied with fine husk. For meat, chicken, pork, and veal are considered the best. There is also a sweet tamale, made with raisins or preserves.

SOME FOOD VARIANTS

The following recipe for tamales was given us by Luna:

TAMALES Boil one chicken until the meat comes from the bones. Chop the meat fine and moisten it with the liquor in which it was boiled. Boil six large chili peppers in a little water until cooked so they can be strained through a fine strainer, and add to this the chopped chicken, with salt to taste and a little chopped parsley. Take corn meal and work into it a lump of butter the size of an egg, adding boiling water and working constantly until it makes a paste the consistency of biscuit dough. Have ready a pile of the soft inner husks of green corn and on each husk spread a lump of dough, the size of a walnut, into a flat cake covering the husk. In the center of the dough put a teaspoonful of the chopped meat with minced olive. On a large husk put several tablespoonfuls of chopped meat with olives. Roll this together and lay on them other husks until the tamale is of the size desired. Tie the ends together with strips of fine husk and put in boiling water for twenty minutes. Either veal or pork may be used instead of chicken.

Polenti, properly prepared, is a dish that requires much labor, and scarcely repays for the time and exertion spent in its making. It differs from scrapple in that the ingredients are mixed in a sauce and poured over the mush instead of being mixed in the meal. In the New Buon Gusto restaurant, in Broadway, they cook polenti to perfection, and when it is served with cippino it leaves nothing to be desired. This is the recipe:

SAN FRANCISCO

POLENTI

For the gravy: Make a little broth with veal bone, a small piece of beef, a pig's foot, neck, feet and gizzard of chicken. In a separate kettle cook in hot oil one sliced onion, one clove of garlic, a little parsley, one bell pepper, one tomato, a small piece of celery, and a carrot. Cook until soft and then add this to the broth with a few dried mushrooms. Cook slowly for thirty minutes and then strain.

For the mush: Boil corn meal until it is thoroughly done and then cool it until it can be cut in slices for frying. Mix butter and olive oil and heat in a frying pan and into this put the slices of corn meal, frying to a light brown. Place the fried corn meal in a platter in layers, sprinkling each with grated Parmesan cheese, salt, and pepper. Take parsley and one clove of garlic chopped fine and a can of French mushrooms cut in quarters, and fry in butter, then add enough gravy to pour over the fried corn meal. Place this in an oven for a few minutes then serve.

BOHEMIAN

ABOUT DINING

Table d'hote is the feature of San Francisco's restaurant life. It is the ideal method for those who wish a good dinner and who have not the inclination, or the knowledge, to order a special dinner. It is also the least expensive way of getting a good dinner. It also saves an exhibition of ignorance regarding the dishes, for if you are in doubt all you have to do is to leave it to the waiter, and he will bring the best there is on the day's menu and will serve it properly.

It is really something to elicit wonder when one considers the possibilities of a table d'hote dinner in some of the less expensive restaurants. Take, for instance, the Buon Gusto, in Broadway. This restaurant boasts a good chef, and the food is the finest the market affords. Here is served a six course dinner for fifty cents, and the menu card is typical of this class of restaurants. What is provided is shown by the following taken from the bill of fare as it was served us:

Hor d'ouvres—four kinds; five kinds of salad; two kinds of soup; seven kinds of fish; four kinds of paste; broiled spring chicken; green salad with French dressing; ice cream or rum omelet; mixed fruits; demi tasse.

With this is served a pint of good table wine.

As one goes up with the scale of prices in the restaurants that charge $1, $1.25, $1.50, $2, $2.50, and $3 for their dinners it will be found that the difference lies chiefly in the variety from which to choose and from the surroundings and service.

Take, for example, the following typical menu for a dollar dinner, served at the Fior d'Italia, and compare it with the fifty-cent dinner just mentioned:

Salami and anchovies; salad; chicken broth with Italian paste; fillet of English sole, sauce tartare; spaghetti or ravioli; escallop of veal, caper sauce; French peas with butter; roast chicken with chiffon salad; ice cream or fried cream; assorted fruits and cakes; demi tasse. Wine with this dinner is extra.

SAN FRANCISCO

Now going a step up in the scale we come to the $1.50 dinner as follows:

ABOUT DINING

Anchovies, salami (note that it is the same as above); combination salad; tortellini di Bologna soup; striped bass a la Livornaise; ravioli a la Genoese and spaghetti with mushrooms; chicken saute, Italian style, with green peas; squab with lettuce; zabaione; fruit; cheese; coffee. Wine is extra.

Let us now look at the menu of the $3.50 dinner, without wine:

Pate de foie gras—truffles on toast; salad; olives; Alice Fallstaff; Italian ham "Prosciutto;" soup—semino Italiani with Brodo de Cappone; pompano a la papillote; tortellini with fungi a funghetto; fritto misto; spring chicken saute; Carcioffi all'Inferno; Capretto al Forno con Insallata; omelet Celestine; fruit; cheese, and black coffee.

This dinner must be ordered three days in advance.

These menus will give a good idea of the different classes of dinners that can be obtained. Between are dinners to suit all tastes and pocketbooks. If you wish to go beyond these there is no limit except the amount of money you have. If but the food value be taken into consideration then one will be as well pleased with the fifty-cent dinner as he will be at the higher priced meals, but if light and music and brilliant surroundings are desired, then one must pay for them as well as for the meal he eats.

All of the restaurants mentioned serve good table d'hote dinners, giving an astonishing variety of foods for the money, and it is all cooked and served in a manner that leaves nothing to be desired. As before mentioned if you wish a table d'hote dinner composed entirely of sea food you can get it at the Shell Fish Grotto for one dollar.

A good rule to follow when dining at any of the restaurants is: When in doubt order a table d'hote dinner. You will always get a good meal, for the least out-

BOHEMIAN

lay of money and least expenditure of thought. Often one desires something a little different, and this is easy, too, and you can conserve your brain energy and get the most for the least money by seeing the proprietor or manager of the restaurant and telling him that you wish to give a little dinner. Tell him how many will be in the party and give him the amount you wish to spend. It will be surprising, sometimes, to see how much more you can get for a slight increase in the price. Of course your wines and cocktails will be extra and these must be reckoned in the cost.

ABOUT DINING

From this we come to the ordered dinner, and here is where your own knowledge and special desires come in. Here, too, comes a marked increase in the cost. You now have the widest range of possibilities both as to viands and as to price. It is not at all difficult to have a dinner, without wine, that costs twenty-five dollars a plate, and when you come down to the more normal dinners, unless you confine yourself to one or two dishes you will find that you far exceed in price the table d'hote dinners of equal gastronomic value.

While this is true it is well to be able to order your dinner for it frequently occurs that one does not care to go through the heavy course dinner provided table d'hote. Sometimes one wants a simple dish, or perhaps two, and it is well to know something about them and how to order them. We have made it a rule whenever we have seen something new on the bill of fare to order it, on the theory that we are willing to try anything once, and in this way we have greatly enlarged our knowledge of good things.

It is also well to remember national characteristics and understand that certain dishes are at their best at certain restaurants. For instance, you will be served with an excellent paste at a French restaurant, but if you want it at its best you will get it at an Italian res-

SAN FRANCISCO

taurant. On the other hand if you desire a delicate entree you will get the best at a French restaurant. For instance, one would not ask for sauerbraten anywhere except at a German restaurant. It will readily be seen that the Elegant Art of Dining in San Francisco means much more than the sitting at table and partaking of what is put before you. Dining is an art, and its pleasure is greatly enhanced by a knowledge of foods, cooking, serving, national characteristics, and combinations of both foods and wines. How few people are there, for instance, who know that one should never drink any hard liquor, like whisky, brandy, or gin, with oysters. Many a fit of acute stomach trouble has been attributed to some food that was either bad or badly prepared when the cause of the trouble was the fact that a cocktail had been taken just prior to eating oysters.

ABOUT DINING

Some of the possibilities of dining in San Francisco may be understood when we tell you of a progressive dinner. We had entertained one of the Exposition Commissioners from a sister State and he was so well pleased with what he had learned in a gastronomic way that he said to us:

"The Governor of my State is coming and I should like to give him a dinner that will open his eyes to San Francisco's possibilities. Would it be asking too much of you to have you help me do it?"

"We shall be glad to. What do you want us to do?"

"Take charge of the whole business, do as you please and go as far as you like."

"That is a wide order, General. What is the limit of price, and how many will be in the party?"

"Just six. That will include the Governor and his wife, you two and myself and wife. Let it be something unusual and do not let the cost interfere. What I want is something unusual."

BOHEMIAN

ABOUT DINING

It has been told us that when the Governor got back home he tried to tell some of his friends about that dinner, but they told him he had acquired the California habit of talking wide. This is the way we carried out the dinner, everything being arranged in advance: At 6:30 we called at the rooms of the Governor in the Palace Hotel and had served there dry Martini cocktails with Russian caviar on toasted rye bread.

An automobile was in waiting, and at seven o'clock we were set down at Felix's, in Montgomery street, where a table was ready for us and on it were served salami of various kinds, artichokes in oil and ripe olives. Then came a service of soup, for which this restaurant is famous, followed by a combination salad, with which was served a bottle of Pontet Canet.

The automobile carried us then over to Broadway and at the Fior d'Italia our table was waiting and here we were served with sand-dabs au gratin, and a small glass of sauterne.

All the haste we made was on the streets, and when we finished our course at the Fior d'Italia we whirled away over toward North Beach to the Gianduja, where had been prepared especially for us tagliarini with chicken livers and mushrooms, and because of its success we had a bottle of Lacrima Christi Spumanti, the enjoyment of which delayed us.

Again in the automobile to Coppa's where Chicken Portola was served, with green peas. Accompanying this was a glass of Krug, and this was followed by a glass of zabaione for dessert.

Back again to the heart of the city and we stopped at Raggi's, in Montgomery street near Commercial where we had a glass of brandy in which was a chinotti (a peculiar Italian preserved fruit which is said to be a cross between a citron and an orange).

SAN FRANCISCO

Then around the corner to Gouailhardou & Rondel's, the Market Cafe, where from a plain pine table, and on sanded floor, we had our coffee royal. As a fitting climax for this evening we directed the chauffeur to drive to the Cliff House, where, over a bottle of Krug, we talked it all over as we watched the dancing and listened to the singing of the cabaret performers.

This dinner, including everything from the automobile to the tips cost but fifteen dollars for each one in the party.

BOHEMIAN

SOMETHING ABOUT COOKING

Cooking is sometimes a pleasure, sometimes a duty, sometimes a burden and sometimes a martyrdom, all according to the point of view. The extremes are rarities, and sometimes duty and burden are synonymous. In ordinary understanding we have American cooking and Foreign cooking, and to one accustomed to plain American cooking, all variants, and all additions of spices, herbs, or unusual condiments is classed under the head of Foreign. In the average American family cooking is a duty usually considered as one of the necessary evils of existence, and food is prepared as it is usually eaten—hastily—something to fill the stomach.

The excuse most frequently heard in San Francisco for the restaurant habit, and for living in cooped-up apartments, is that the wife wants to get away from the burden of the kitchen and drudgery of housework. And like many other effects this eventually becomes a cause, for both husband and wife become accustomed to better cooking than they could get at home and there is a continuance of the custom, for both get a distaste for plainly cooked food, and the wife does not know how to cook any other way.

Yet when all is considered the difference between plain American cooking and what is termed Foreign cooking, is but the proper use of condiments and seasoning, combined with proper variety of the food supply from the markets. Herein lies the secret of a good table—proper combination of ingredients and proper variation and selection of the provisions together with proper preparation and cooking of the food.

We have met with many well educated and well raised men and women whose gastronomic knowledge was so limited as to be appalling. All they knew of meats was confined to ordinary poultry, i. e., chickens and turkeys, and to beef, veal, pork, and mutton. Of

SAN FRANCISCO

SOMETHING ABOUT COOKING

these there were but three modes of cooking—frying, stewing and baking, sometimes boiling. Their chops were always fried as they knew nothing of the delicate flavor imparted by broiling. In fact their knowledge was confined to the least healthful and least nutritious modes of preparation and cooking. Not only is this true of the average American family, but their lack of knowledge of the fundamentals of cooking and food values brings about a waste largely responsible for what is called the "high cost of living." It is a trite, but nevertheless true saying that a French family could live well on what an American family wastes. Waste in preparation is but the mildest form of waste. Waste consequent upon lack of knowledge of food values is the waste that is doubly expensive for it not only wastes food but it also wastes the system whose energy is exhausted in trying to assimilate improper alimentation.

It is a well recognized medical fact that much of the illness of Americans arises from two causes, improper food and improper eating methods. In Europe this fact was recognized and generally known so long ago that the study of food values and preparation for proper assimilation is one of the essential parts of every woman's education, and to such a degree has this become raised to a science that schools and even colleges in cooking are to be found in many parts of England, France and Germany. Francatelli, the great chef who was at the head of Queen Victoria's kitchen, boasts proudly of his diploma from the Parisian College of Cooking.

The United States is now beginning to wake up to the fact that the preparation of food is something more than a necessary evil, and from the old cooking classes of our common schools has developed the classes in Domestic Science, that which was formerly considered drudgery now being elevated to an art and dignified as

BOHEMIAN

SOMETHING ABOUT COOKING

a science. In Europe this stage was reached many generations ago, and there it is now an art which has elevated the primitive process of feeding to the elegant art of dining. In San Francisco probably more than in any other city in the United States, not even excepting New Orleans, this art has flourished for many years with the result that the average San Franciscan is disappointed at the food served in other cities of his country, and always longs for his favorite restaurant even as the children of Israel longed for the flesh pots of Egypt.

One needs to spend a day in the Italian quarter of San Francisco to come to a full realization of the difference between the requirements of even the poorest Italian family and the average American family of the better class. We need but say that we have been studying this question for nearly twenty years yet even now we meet with surprises in the way of new delicacies and modes of using herbs and spices in food preparation.

If we were to attempt even to enumerate the various herbs, spices, flavorings, delicacies, and pastes to be found in a well regulated Italian shop it would take many pages of this book, yet every one of these articles has its own individual and peculiar use, and the knowledge of these articles and how to use them is what makes the difference between American and Foreign cooking. Each herb has a peculiar quality as a stomachic and it must be as delicately measured as if it were a medicine. The use of garlic, so much decried as plebeian, is the secret of some of the finest dishes prepared by the highest chefs. It must not be forgotten that in the use of all flavors and condiments there may be an intemperance, there lying the root of much of the bad cooking.

Garlic, for instance, is a flavor and not a food, yet many of the lower class foreigners eat it on bread, mak-

SAN FRANCISCO

ing a meal of dark bread, garlic and red wine. It is offensive to sensitive nostrils and vitiates the taste when thus used, but when properly added to certain foods it gives an intangible flavor which never fails to elicit praise. What is true of garlic is also true of the many herbs that are used.

SOMETHING ABOUT COOKING

It is easy to pass from a rare flavor that makes a most savory dish to a taste of medicine that spoils a dinner. With the well-known prodigal and wasteful habits of America the American who learns the use of herbs usually makes the initial mistake of putting in the flavoring herbs with too lavish a hand, and it is only after years of experience that a knowledge of proper combinations is obtained.

Visitors have often expressed wonder at the variety of foods and delicate flavors in San Francisco restaurants, and possibly this brief explanation may give some comprehension of why San Franciscans always want to get back to where they "can get something to eat."

BOHEMIAN

TOLD IN A WHISPER

"Surely the old Bohemians of San Francisco did not spend all their time in restaurants. How did they live when at home?" This is what was said to us one day when we were talking about the old days and the old people. Indeed they did not live all their time in restaurants. Some of the most enjoyable meals we have eaten have been in the rooms and apartments of our Bohemian friends, and these meals were prepared generally by each one present doing his or her part in making it a success. One would make the salad, another the main dish, and others do various forms of scullery work, and in the end we would have a meal that would often put to blush the efforts of many of the renowned chefs.

Many people who come to San Francisco will wish to conserve their finances as much as possible, and they will wish to enjoy life in their apartments. There are also many people who live in San Francisco who need a little advice on how to get the best out of life, and we are going to whisper a few words to all such as these we have mentioned.

You can be a Bohemian and have the very best sort of living in your own room for less than half the money it will take to live at the hotels and restaurants, and we are sure many of you would like to know something about how to do it. It is not necessary to confine yourself to the few things in your limited experience. If you are going to be in San Francisco for more than a week, you will find that a little apartment, furnished ready for housekeeping, will give you opportunity to be independent and free. You will get your own breakfasts, when and how you want them. Your luncheons and dinners can be gotten in your rooms or at the restaurants just as you are inclined.

You will find delight and education in visiting the markets, and the foreign stores where all the strange

SAN FRANCISCO

and unusual foods of all nations are to be found. You will discover better articles at less prices at the little Italian, French, Mexican or Chinese stores and stalls than can be had in the most aristocratic stores in the city. Above all you will find a joy of invention and will be surprised at the delectable dishes you can prepare at a minimum of cost.

TOLD IN A WHISPER

When you visit San Francisco you are desirous of so arranging your finances that you may see the most for the least outlay of money. After a strenuous day of sight-seeing you will scarcely feel like getting up a good meal, consequently then you will follow the ideas suggested in this book and visit the various restaurants, thus obtaining a variety both in foods and in information of an educational nature. But sometimes you will not be tired, or you will wish to get up a little late supper after theatre, and it is then that you will be glad of the opportunity afforded by having your own kitchen arrangements so that you can carry out your tastes, and cook some of the strange and new foods that you have discovered in your rambles through the foreign quarters.

Take the simple matter of sausage, for instance. Ordinarily we know of but three kinds—pork sausage, frankfurter and bologna—neither very appetizing or appealing, except sometimes the pork sausage for breakfast. Over in the little Italian and French shops you will find some of the most wonderful sausages that mind can conceive of. Some of these are so elaborate in their preparation that they cost even in that inexpensive part of the city, seventy cents a pound, and the variety is almost as infinite as that of the pastes. In the Mexican stores you will find a sausage that gives a delightful flavor to anything it is cooked with, and it is when you see these sausages that your eyes begin to be opened.

BOHEMIAN

You now take cognizance of many things that heretofore escaped your observation. You see new canned goods; a wonderful variety of cheeses; strange dried vegetables and delicacies unheard of; preserved vegetables and fish and meats in oil; queer fish pickled and dried. You begin to learn of the many uses of olive oil in cooking and in food preparation. You see the queer shapes of bread, and note the numerous kinds of cakes and pastry that you never saw or heard of before. You see boxes of dried herbs, and begin to realize why you have never been able to reproduce certain flavors you have tasted in restaurants. You see strange-looking, flat hams, and are told that they are Italian hams, and if you buy some you will find that they cut the ham the wrong way, and instead of slicing it across the grain they cut in very thin slices down the length of the bone. Their flavor is more delicious than that of any ham you have tasted since you used to get the old-time, genuine country smoked hams. But if you investigate a little deeper you will learn that these hams were not put up in Italy at all, but that it is a special brand that is prepared in Virginia for the Italians.

In the French stores you will find preserved cockscombs, snails, marvelous blood sausages with nuts in them, rare cheeses, prepared meats in jellies, and hundreds of delicacies unknown to you. You can spend days in these stores, finding something new all the time. We have been going there for years and still run across new things.

Remember that to the people of the Latin Quarter these things are all usual consequently they think you know as much about them as they do, and will volunteer no information regarding them. Possibly they will smile at your ignorance when you ask them questions, but do not hesitate to ask, for they are courteous and

TOLD IN A WHISPER

SAN FRANCISCO

that is the only way you can find out things, and learn what all these new edibles are and what they are good for. There is no greater possibility of interest than is to be found in the stores of San Francisco's Latin Quarter, and we mean by this the stores that cater to the people of the Quarter. In stores and restaurants frequented by Americans they cater to American tastes and lose much of the foreign flavor.

TOLD IN A WHISPER

It is also well to bear in mind that it is not in the largest stores that you find the greatest variety when it comes to odd and new goods. A little shop, barely large enough to turn around in between counter and wall, may have enough of interest to entertain you for half an hour, and here the prices will be remarkably low, for these people have so little of the outside trade that they have not learned to add to their prices when they see an American face coming.

What is true of the stores is also true of the vegetable stands, the meat shops, the fish stalls, and bakeries. Here you will find better and fresher food supplies than in any of the similar places in other parts of the city, and the price is generally one-third less. The high cost of living has not reached this thrifty people with their inborn knowledge of the values of foods. They live twice as well as the average American family at half the cost. They combine knowledge of food values with the art of preparation and have a resultant meal that is tasty, full flavored, and nourishing at a minimum of expense.

Perhaps you want a meal. Your thoughts at once run to steaks and chops, and fried potatoes. Nothing but a porterhouse or tenderloin steak or a kidney chop will do. It is the most expensive meat and you think that of course it is the best and most nourishing. If the knowledge of food values were with you, you would get

113

BOHEMIAN

the less expensive and more nourishing cuts. A flank steak, perhaps, prepared en casserole, and you would have a fine dish for half the money. As it is in meats so it is in all foods. For ten cents two people can have a dinner of tagliarini that is at once nourishing and satisfying in flavor. Of course all this requires knowledge, but that is easily acquired, and it adds to the zest of life to know that you can do that which lifts eating from the plane of feeding to that of dining; that you can change existence into living. All because you dare to break away from conventionalities which make so many people affect ignorance of how to live because they imagine it is an evidence of refinement. If they but knew it, their affectation and their ignorance is the hall mark of low caste.

Now about this whisper: We have a friend who has a little apartment where he has kept bachelor's hall for many years. Here some of our most pleasant evenings have been spent, and we never fear to go on account of the possibility that he may be embarrassed or inconvenienced through lack of something to eat or drink, for he is never at a loss to prepare something dainty and appetizing for us, and it really seems, sometimes, that he makes a meal out of nothing. Often Charlie telephones us that he has discovered a new dish and hurries us over to pass judgment on it. And, by the way, many of the good dishes of Bohemia are the result of accident rather than design.

SAN FRANCISCO

It is surprising what a good meal you can get up sometimes when "there's not a thing in the house to eat." Let us give you an example. One evening two of our young friends came over to tell us their sweet secret, and with them was another young lady. OUT OF NOTHING
While we were talking it over and making plans for the wedding another friend dropped in because he said our "light looked inviting."

An hour or so of talk and then one of us signalled to the other and received the shocking signal back, "There's not a thing to eat in the house." This called for an investigation of the larder in which all joined with the following result: Item—two cans of reed birds from China, each containing twelve of the little birds as large as your thumb. Item—one egg. Other items— one onion, two slices of dry bread, one green pepper, rather small, one dozen crackers. Item—one case of imported Italian Vin d'Oro Spumanti. Item—six hearty appetites to be appeased.

The gentleman who saw our light saw another, and rushed off to a barber shop, and got four more eggs. Barbers use eggs, and they must be fresh ones, in shampooing, and our friend remembered it.

The two young ladies and the young man prepared the table, and the other lady and the two gentlemen set about getting a meal. One of us made an omelet of the five eggs, the onion and the green pepper, with crumbs of bread, and this is the recipe:

Take five eggs and beat until very light. Roll two slices of dried bread to crumbs and mix with the beaten eggs. Chop fine OMELET A LA PERUQUIER
one onion and one green pepper, season with salt and pepper. Pour a tablespoonful of olive oil in an omelet pan and in this fry the peppers and onion to a light brown. When ready turn into this the beaten eggs, and cook until done. Follow the rule of never disturbing a cooking egg or a sleeping child. Serve on a hot dish.

BOHEMIAN

Take two cans of Chinese reed birds, open them and take therefrom the two dozen birds contained therein. In a hot frying pan place the birds in the grease that comes around them and heat them through. Toast twelve square crackers and on each place two reed birds, and serve two on each of six hot plates. With both the omelet and the reed birds serve Vin d'Oro.

REED BIRDS A LA CHINOISE

SAN FRANCISCO

In an Italian grocery store we noticed a great variety of pastes in boxes arranged along the counter and began counting them. The proprietor noticed us and, with a characteristic shrug of his shoulders, said: "That is but a few of them. We have not room to show them all." In response to our inquiry regarding the number of kinds of paste made by Italians he said there were more than seventy-five. Ordinarily we think of one—spaghetti—or possibly two, including macaroni. If our knowledge goes a little farther we think also of tagliarini, which is the Italian equivalent of noodles, as it is made with eggs.

PASTE MAKES WAIST

In New York we were much impressed with the stress they laid on the serving of spaghetti, and one restaurant went so far as to advertise dinners given "under the spaghetti vine." It appears that this is the only paste they know anything about.

After one eats tagliarini or ravioli one feels like paraphrasing the darkey and saying, "go way spaghetti, yo done los' yo tase."

Then comes tortelini which, like ravioli, combines paste with meat and spinach. These may be considered the most prominent of the pastes, the others being variants in the making and cutting, each serving a special purpose in cooking, some being for soups, others for sauces and others for dressing for meats. It is more than probable that the great variety comes from individual tastes in cutting or rolling.

All Italian restaurants serve the paste as a releve rather than as an entree, which it usually follows, preceding the roast in the dinner. As a separate and distinct dish it can well be made to serve as a full meal, especially when tagliarini is prepared after the following recipe:

Cook one pound of tagliarini in boiling water twenty-five minutes, then draw off the water. To the tagliarini add a hand-

BOHEMIAN

TAGLIARINI
DES
BEAUX ARTS

ful of mushrooms which have been sliced and fried in butter. Then add three chicken livers which have been chopped small and fried, one sliced truffle, one red pepper chopped fine and a little Parmesan cheese. Make a brown sauce of one-third beef broth thickened with melted butter and flour and two-thirds tomato sauce, and pour this over the tagliarini. Sprinkle with the Parmesan cheese and serve very hot from a chafing dish. (By Oliver, chef of the Restaurant des Beaux Arts, Paris.)

In San Francisco one finds both the imported and the domestic paste, and frequently one hears the assertion that the imported is the better. This idea is born of the thought that all things from Europe are better than the same made in America. In fact the paste that comes from Italy is neither so good in taste, nor is it so clean in the making. We have visited a number of paste factories in San Francisco and have found them all scrupulously clean, with the best of materials in the composition of the pastes.

One often wonders how the pastes came to be so many and how they received their names. Names of some of them are accidents, as is illustrated by macaroni. According to an Italian friend who vouches for the fact, it received its name from an expression of pleasure. "Macari" means "fine, excellent," and the superlative is "macaroni." A famous Italian gourmet constantly desired new dishes to please his taste, and one day his chef carried to him something that was unusual. The gourmet tasted it, cried out "macari!" Tasted again, threw out his arms in delight and cried "macaroni!"

"What is the name of this wonderful dish?"

"You have named it. It is macaroni."

SAN FRANCISCO

TIPS AND TIPPING

Tipping is variously designated. Some say it is a nuisance and should be abolished. Some call it an outrage and ask for legislative interference. Some say it is an extortion and refuse to pay it. Some say it is a necessary evil and suffer it. The wise ones look at it a little differently. Possibly it is best explained or excused, whichever way you wish to call it, by one of Gouverneur Morris's characters in a recent story, who says:

"Whenever I go anywhere I find persons in humble situations who smile at me and wish me well. I smile back and wish them well. It is because at some time or other I have tipped them. To me the system has never been an annoyance but a delightful opportunity for the exercise of tact and judgment."

We look upon tipping as a part of expense to be calculated upon, necessary to insure good service, not only now but in the future, and it should always be computed in the expense of a trip or a dinner. Tipping, to our minds, is the oil that makes the wheels of life run smoothly.

The amount of the tip is always a matter of individual judgment, dependent upon the service rendered, and the way it is rendered. The good traveler wants to tip properly, neither too little nor too much, thereby getting the best service, for in the last analysis the pleasure of a trip depends upon the service received. American prodigality and asininity is responsible for much of the abuse of tipping. Too many Americans when they travel desire to appear important and the only way they can accomplish this is by buying the subserviency of menials who laugh at them behind their backs.

A tip should always depend upon the service rendered. We make it a rule to withhold the tip from a careless or inconsiderate waiter, and always add to the tip a word of commendation when there has been extra

BOHEMIAN

good service. The amount of the tip depends, first on the service, second on the amount of the bill, and third, on the character of the place where you are served. When we order a specially prepared dinner, with our suggestions as to its composition and service, we tip the head waiter, the chef, the waiter and the bus boy. We have given dinners where the tips amounted to fully half as much as the dinner itself, and we felt that this part of the expense brought us the greatest pleasure.

TIPS AND TIPPING

It is impossible to make a hard and fast rule regarding how much to give a waiter. Each person must use his or her own judgment. If you are in a foreign country you might do as we did on our first trip to Paris. We wanted to do what was right but not what most Americans think is right. We were at a hotel where only French were usually guests, and in order to do the right thing we took the proprietor into our confidence and explained to him our dilemma. We asked him whom to tip and how much to give, and he got us out of our difficulty and we found that the tips amounted to about as much for one whole week as we had been held up for in one day at the Waldorf-Astoria.

SAN FRANCISCO

Notwithstanding the fact that Webster gives no recognition in his dictionary to the Land of Bohemia or the occupants thereof, the land exists, perhaps not in a material way, but certainly mentally. Some have not the perception to see it; some know not the language that admits entrance; some pass it by every day without understanding it. Yet it as truly exists as any of the lands told of in our childhood fables and fairy stories.

THE MYTHICAL LAND

The old definition of Bohemian was "a vagabond, a wayfarer." Possibly that definition may, to a certain extent, be true of the present-day Bohemian, for he is a mental vagabond and a mental wayfarer.

In our judgment the word comes from the French "Bon Homme," for surely the Bohemian is a "good man."

Whatever may be the derivation the fact remains that not to all is given the perception to understand, nor the eyes to see, and therein lies one of the dangers of writing such a book as this. If you read this and then hurry off to a specified restaurant with the expectation of finding the Bohemian atmosphere in evidence you are apt to be disappointed, for frequently it is necessary to create your own Bohemian atmosphere.

Then, too, all nights are not the same at restaurants. For instance if you desire the best service afforded in any restaurant do not select Saturday or Sunday night, but if you will lay aside your desire for personal comfort in service, and wish to study character, then take Saturday or Sunday night for your visit. It is very possible that you will think the restaurant has changed hands between Friday and Saturday. On Saturday and Sunday evening the mass of San Francisco's great cosmopolitan population holds holiday and the great feature of the holiday is a restaurant dinner, where there is music, and glitter, and joyous, human

APPENDIX

HOW TO SERVE WINES

A few hints regarding the proper serving of wines may not be amiss, and we give you here the consensus of opinion of the most noted gourmets who have made a study of the best results from combinations:

Never drink any hard liquors, such as whisky, brandy, gin, or cocktails, with oysters or clams, as it is liable to upset you for the rest of the evening.

With the hor d'ouvres serve vermouth, sherry, marsala or madeira wine.

With soup and fish serve white wines, such as Rhein wine, sauterne or white burgundy.

With entrees serve clarets or other red wines, such as Swiss, Bordeaux, Hungarian or Italian wines.

Burgundy may also be served at any of the later courses.

With roasts serve champagne or any of the sparkling wines.

With the coffee serve kirsch, French brandy or fine champagne.

After coffee serve a liqueur. Never serve more than one glass of any liqueur.

The following wines may be considered the best types:
Amontillado, Montilo and Olorosa sherries.

Austrian burgundy is one of the finest wines, possessing rich flavor and fine perfume.

Other burgundies are:
Chablis: A white burgundy, dry and of agreeable aroma.
Chambertin: A sound, delicate wine with a flavor resembling raspberry.
Clos de Vogeot: Similar to chambertin, and often called the king of burgundy.
Romanee: A very rare and costly wine of rich, ruby color, with a delicate bouquet.

Clarets are valued for their flavor and for their tonic properties. Some of the best are:
Chateau Grille: A dessert wine of good flavor and fine aroma.
Chateau Lafitte: Has beautiful color and delicate flavor.
Chateau la Rose: Greater alcoholic strength and of fine flavor.
Chateau Margaux: Rich, with delicate flavor and excellent bouquet.
Pontet Canet: A heavier wine with good bouquet and fine flavor.
St. Julien: A lighter claret with good bouquet.

HOW TO SERVE WINES

German wines are of lighter character, and are generally termed Rhein wines. The best varieties are:

Hochheimer: A light, pleasing and wholesome wine.

Brauneberger: A good variety with pleasing flavor and aroma.

Dreimanner: Similar to Brauneberger.

Deidesheimer: Similar to Brauneberger.

Graffenberg: Light and pleasant. Good aroma.

Johannisberger Schloss: One of the best of the German wines.

Rudesheimer Schloss: In class with Johannisberger.

Italian wines are mostly red, the most noted in California being Chianti, and its California prototype, Tipo Chianti, made by the Asti Colony.

Lacrima Christi Spumanti: The finest Italian champagne. Dry and of magnificent bouquet.

Vin d'Oro Spumanti: A high-class champagne. Sweet and of fine bouquet and flavor.

Lacrima Christi: A still wine of excellent flavor and bouquet.

Malaga: A wine of high repute. Sweet and powerful. A peculiar flavor is given to it through the addition of a small quantity of burned wine.

Marsala: Is a golden wine of most agreeable color and aroma.

Sauterne: Is a white Bordeaux, a strong luscious wine, the best known varieties being:

Chateau Yquem: Remarkable for its rich and velvety softness.

Barsac: Rich and good.

Chateau Filhot: Of rich color and good flavor.

Chateau Latour Blanche: A white sauterne of exquisite bouquet.

Haut Sauterne: Soft and mild. Of good flavor.

Vin de Graves: Good and strong. Good aroma and flavor.

Vintage years have much to do with the quality of wines. The best vintage years are as follows:

Champagnes: 1892.
Rhein and Moselle: 1893.
Burgundy: 1892, 1899 and 1904.
Claret: 1898 and 1904.
Port: 1896 and 1904.
Sherry: 1882, 1890, 1898 and 1900.

A GOOD BOHEMIAN DINNER

Sometimes people desire to give a dinner and are at loss as to the proper time to serve wines. The following menu will give some ideas on the subject:

MENU

Gibson Cocktail   Canape Norwegian
(Serve these before entering dining room)

Artichoke Hearts in Oil   Ripe Olives   Celery

Amontillado Sherry

Oysters on Half Shell

Bisque of Ecrevisse   Chablis, or White Sauterne

Sand-dabs Edward VII   Sliced Cucumbers, Iced

Escargot Francais   Chateau Lafitte

Cassolette of Terrapin, Maryland   Romanee

Tagliarini des Beaux Arts

Punch Pistache   Cigarettes

Alligator Pears with Cumquats, French Dressing

Chicken Portola   Krug Private Cuvee Brut

Creamed New Potatoes   Celery Victor   French Peas

Zabaione

Reina Cabot

Coffee Royal   Cigarettes

Grand Marnier

A FEW RARE RECIPES

In our travels through Bohemia it has been our good fortune to gather hundreds of recipes of new, strange and rare dishes, prepared by those who look farther than the stoking of the physical system in the preparation of foods. Some of these are from chefs in restaurants and hotels, some from men and women of the foreign colonies and some from good friends who lent their aid in our pleasurable occupation. That we cannot print them all in a volume of this size is our regret, but another book now in preparation will contain them, together with other talks about San Francisco's foreign quarters.

From our store we have selected the following as being well worth trying:

ONION SOUP

Cut four large onions in large pieces and put them in six ounces of butter with pepper and salt. Slowly stew this in a little beef stock and a little milk, stirring constantly, for one hour. Add more stock and milk and let cook slowly for another hour. In a tureen place slices of bread sprinkled with two tablespoonfuls of Parmesan cheese. Beat the yolks of four eggs and mix them with a tablespoonful of the soup and pour this over the bread and cheese. Cover this for five minutes and then pour over it the rest of the soup.

CREOLE GUMBO SOUP

Take two young chickens, cut in pieces, roll in flour and fry to light brown. Take the fried chicken, a ham bone stripped of meat for flavor, a tablespoonful of chopped thyme, of rosemary, two bay leaves, a sprig of tarragon and boil in four quarts of water until the meat loosens from the bones. Slice and fry brown two large onions and add two heaping quarts of sliced okra and one cut up pod of red pepper. Stir all over the fire until the okra is thoroughly wilted then remove the larger bones and let cook three quarters of an hour before serving. Half an hour before serving add a can of tomatoes or an equal quantity of fresh ones, and a pint of shrimps, boiled and shredded. Have a dish of well boiled and dry rice and serve with two or three tablespoonfuls in each soup plate.

OYSTER SALAD

To a solid pint of oysters use a dressing made as follows: Beat well two eggs and add to them half a gill each of cream and vinegar, half teaspoonful mustard, celery seed, salt each, one-tenth teaspoonful cayenne, and a tablespoonful of butter. Put all in a double boiler and cook until it all is as thick as soft custard (about six minutes), stirring constantly. Take from

A FEW RARE RECIPES

the fire. Heat the oysters in their own liquor to a boiling point then drain and add the dressing, mixing lightly. Set away in cold place until needed.

ITALIAN SALAD — Soak two salt herrings in milk over night and then remove the bones and skin and cut up in small pieces. Cut in small pieces one and one-half pounds each of cold roast veal and cold boiled tongue and add to these and the herrings six boiled potatoes, half a dozen small cucumber pickles and two small boiled beets, all cut up, and two raw apples, three boiled carrots and one large boiled celery root, all minced. Mix all the above in salad bowl and pour over it mayonnaise dressing. Garnish the tops with hard boiled eggs, sliced, and capers, and ripe olives from which the stones have been removed. Garnish the bowl with parsley and in the center put hard boiled eggs stuffed with capers.

SOLARI'S CRAB LOUIS — Take meat of crab in large pieces and dress with the following: One-third mayonnaise, two-thirds chili sauce, small quantity chopped English chow-chow, a little Worcestershire sauce and minced tarragon, shallots and sweet parsley. Season with salt and pepper and keep on ice.

SOLES WITH WINE — Take fillets of sole and pound lightly with blade of knife then soak them two hours in beaten eggs seasoned with salt and pepper. When ready to cook roll them in bread crumbs and fry in olive oil. Take a little of that oil and put in another pan with a tablespoonful of butter and season with salt and pepper and again cook fish in this, adding half a glass of dry white wine. Sprinkle with chopped parsley and let cook five minutes. Sprinkle with Parmesan cheese and put slices of lemon around it. Serve on hot plates.

GRILLED MUSHROOMS — Skin and remove stalks from large fresh mushrooms and lay on a dish with a little fine olive oil, pepper, and salt, over them for one hour. Broil on a gridiron over a clear sharp fire and serve them with the following sauce:

MUSHROOM SAUCE — Mince the stalks or any spare pieces of mushrooms fine, put in a stewpan with a little broth, some chopped parsley, young onions, butter and the juice of a lemon, or instead of the latter the yolk of an egg beaten up in cream. Beat all together and pour around the mushrooms.

A FEW RARE RECIPES

ITALIAN TURTA Cut very fine the tender part of one dozen artichokes. Take one loaf of stale bread crumbs, moisten and squeeze, and add three tablespoonfuls of grated cheese, three cloves of garlic, bruised, one onion chopped fine, several sprigs of parsley chopped fine, a little celery and half a cup of olive oil. Mix all together thoroughly with plenty of pepper and salt and make into a loaf. Bake slowly forty-five minutes.

OEUFS AU SOLIEL Poach eight fresh eggs then take them out and place in cold water until cool; lay them for a quarter of an hour to marinade in a glass of white wine with sweet herbs. Dry on a cloth and dip in a batter of flour mixed with equal quantities of ale and water to the consistency of double cream. Fry to light brown.

EGGS WITH WINE Put three cupfuls of red wine into a casserole and add three tablespoonfuls of sugar, rind of half a lemon, raisins, and sweet almonds, blanched and chopped. When the wine boils break the eggs into it as in poaching eggs. Let them cook well and then put in serving dish. Add one tablespoonful of flour to the wine and cook to a cream then pour over the eggs.

ITALIAN RISOTTO Soak two level teacups of rice. Mash two cloves of garlic and mix with a little minced parsley. Soak a dozen dried mushrooms in a little water until soft, then chop fine and drain. Cover the bottom of a saucepan with olive oil, place over the fire until quite hot, then put in the garlic, parsley, and mushrooms, add half a can of tomatoes and cook half an hour. Drain the rice and put in a saucepan, adding a little broth, half a cup at a time, to keep from burning, and add, stirring constantly, the other ingredients, cooking all together until the rice is done. Salt to taste; sprinkle with Parmesan cheese.

SCALLOPS OF SWEETBREAD Parboil the sweetbreads and then glaze in reduced Allemande sauce. Dip in bread crumbs and fry in butter until a light brown. When done dish in close order and fill center with Toulouse Ragout, as follows:

TOULOUSE RAGOUT Prepare half a dozen fine, large cockscombs, two dozen button mushrooms, small pieces of sweetbreads and a proportionate quantity of truffles. Place all in a stewpan and add a small ladleful of drawn butter sauce, and the juice of a lemon. Cook a few minutes.

A FEW RARE RECIPES

LAMB CHOPS MARINADE — Soak kidney lamb chops in the following mixture for twelve hours and then broil: Four tablespoonfuls olive oil, one tablespoonful tarragon vinegar, one small sliced onion, one mashed clove of garlic, one broken up bay leaf, twelve whole black peppers, six cloves, one saltspoon of salt, two teaspoonfuls dried thyme, strips of parsley and lemon peel.

SPANISH CHICKEN PIE — Cut up a chicken and boil until tender. Cut up and fry in chicken fat two onions, two green peppers, stirring in one and one-half tablespoonfuls of flour. Have ready five tomatoes, stewed, and put in two dozen ripe olives with a small clove of garlic, mashed. Grate seven large ears of corn, season with salt and put a layer in a greased baking pan, then chicken, then the other ingredients, with a little of the gravy. Stir all together and bake until brown.

CHICKEN JAMBALAYA — Cut a young chicken into small pieces and stew until tender, having the meat covered with the broth when done. Remove the meat, drain and fry to light brown with two slices of onion. Put in the chicken, onion, and one hundred California oysters, back into the broth and season with salt, pepper, juice of a lemon, bruised clove of garlic, chopped green pepper, and a pinch of red pepper. Let all come to a boil. Wash and dry two cups of rice and put into the soup and cook until thoroughly done and moderately dry (twenty-five minutes). Serve hot or cold.

QUAJATALE EN MOLE — This is Mexican Turkey in Red Pepper, a favorite banquet dish. Cut a young turkey into small pieces and boil with shallots and salt. Take half a pound of red peppers, scalded and seeded, and grind fine with black peppers, celery seed, cloves, allspice, and mustard (about half a teaspoonful of each) and add to this some of the broth in which the turkey was cooked. Put a pound of lard in a skillet and, when boiling, put in the mixture with the turkey and let cook ten minutes, sending it to the table hot.

DELMONICO RAISIN SAUCE — Brown butter in a skillet and stir in a teaspoonful of flour, forming a smooth paste. Add one cup of hot soup stock, stirring constantly. While boiling put into this a handful of raisins, handful of blanched almonds, pounded, half a lemon, sliced thin, a few cloves, a pinch of cinnamon, and a little horseradish. Fine for roast beef.

A FEW RARE RECIPES

POULET A LA NAPOLI Cut and trim a chicken as for fricassee. Take the wings, drumsticks, thighs and two pieces of the breast and steep them in cold water half an hour. Drain and wipe dry and dust over with flour and set aside.

Take the rest of the chicken with the giblets and chop small. With water let this simmer for two hours, making a strong broth with a little veal (two ounces or more). Slice an onion into rings which place in the bottom of a stewpan with an ounce of butter. To this add the meat and giblets and a pint of white broth. Let all simmer but not boil or let color. Over this pour common broth until covered and bring slowly to boiling point. Add a small bouquet of herbs and simmer for an hour, then strain. Thicken a little and then simmer in this the stalks and peelings of a quarter of a pound of mushrooms and the chicken that was previously prepared and dusted with flour. When done strain them and drain the chicken. Strain the sauce and thicken with flour until it is of the consistency of a rather thin batter.

Dip the pieces of chicken into the batter until well coated and set aside until it is cold. Then dip the chicken into wellbeaten eggs and cover with bread crumbs. Let set and then repeat. In hot olive oil fry the chicken until a golden brown. Serve on a napkin and garnish with parsley and potatoes Duchesse. Cook the peeled mushrooms in the remaining sauce before the last thickening, and serve in gravy boat to pour over the chicken.

ZABAIONE Beat together, hard, for six minutes, six eggs and four teaspoonfuls of powdered sugar in a double boiler and place over a gentle fire, never ceasing to whip until the contents become stiff enough to sustain a coffee spoon upright in the middle. While whipping add three wineglassfuls of Marsala and one liqueur glass of Maraschino brandy. Pour into tall glasses or cups and serve either hot or cold.

PEACHES A LA PRINCESSE Halve six fine peaches, not too ripe, and place in saucepan with concave side up. Take one peach, peeled, and mince with a dozen macaroons, adding the yolk of an egg and half an ounce of sugar. Mix all well together and with this fill the half peaches. Moisten all with half a cup of white wine and sprinkle with sugar. Bake in a hot oven ten minutes and pour over zabaione and serve. This will make a most delicious dessert dish.

A FEW RARE RECIPES

SULTANA ROLL — Add the beaten yolks of seven eggs to one pint of boiling milk, one cup of sugar, one-half teaspoonful of vanilla, one-quarter teaspoonful of almond extract. When thick add two and a half cups of thick cream. Cool and freeze. Line the bottom of a mold with Sultana raisins which have been soaked in sherry wine twenty-four hours. Put a layer of frozen cream, then raisins, continuing until all is used. Pack in ice and salt two hours and serve with caramel sauce.

CARAMEL SAUCE — Butter the inside of a saucepan. Put in two ounces of unsweetened chocolate and melt over hot water. Add two cups of light brown sugar and mix well. Add one ounce of butter and half a cup of rich milk. Cook until mixture forms a soft ball when tested in cold water. Flavor with vanilla and pour, while hot, over each service of the roll. It immediately hardens, forming a delicious caramel covering to the ice cream.

WELSH RAREBIT — Take one pound of mild American cheese and put in saucepan. Add five wineglassful of old ale, place over the fire and stir until it is thoroughly blended and melted. Pour this over slices of delicately browned toast, serving hot.

COFFEE ROYAL — Take of the best Mocha coffee one part, of the best Java coffee two parts. Put six tablespoonfuls of the mixture into a bowl and add an egg, well beaten. Stir the mixture five minutes. Add half a cup of cold water, cover tightly and let stand several hours. Put into a coffeepot the coffee mixture and add four large cups of boiling water, stirring constantly. Let it boil briskly for five minutes only then set on the back of the stove five minutes. Before serving add a small tablespoonful of pure French brandy to each cup. Sweeten to taste.

REINA CABOT — Mix at table and serve on hot, toasted Bent's biscuit. Take a quarter of a pound of ripe, dark Roquefort cheese and rub with a piece of butter the size of a walnut until smooth, adding a teaspoonful of Worcestershire sauce and a wineglassful of sherry, with a pinch of paprika, rubbing until it is smooth. This is best mixed in shallow bowl or soup plate.

VIRGINIA EGG NOGG — Beat separately the yolks and whites of ten eggs, the yolks to a soft cream. To the beaten yolks add one pound of granulated sugar, beating until fully blended and very light. Let one quart of fresh milk come to a boil and pour over the yolk of

A FEW RARE RECIPES

egg and sugar, stirring constantly until well blended. To this add one gill of French brandy or one-half pint of good whisky. On top of this place the beaten white of egg and grated nutmeg. Serve either hot or cold.

MINT
JULEP

Bruise several sprigs of mint in a mixing glass with pulverized sugar. Fill the glass with ice and pour over it a jigger of whisky. Let stand for ten minutes and then put in a dash of Jamaica rum. Dress with sprigs of mint, and sprinkle with powdered sugar. Serve with straws.

INDEX

Bills of Fare	100, 101, 129
Beefsteak Spanish	9
Celery Victor	64
Chicken, Country Style	65
In the Shell	11
Jambalaya	133
Leon d'Oro	53
A la Napoli	134
Pie (Spanish)	133
Portola	38
Chili Rienas	32
Clam Fritters	92
Chowder	92
Coffee Royal	135
Crab Louis	131
Stew	88
Dessert (Italian)	75
Egg Nog (Virginia)	135
Eggs, Spanish	9
With Wine	132
Des Soliel	132
Fish: Soles with Wine	131
Sole Edward VII	64
Sand-dab Fillet, Cold	61
Fritto Misto	51
Lobster a la Newburg	86
Lamb Chops Marinade	133
Mussels Mariniere	93
Mushrooms, Grilled	131
Mint Julep	136
Menu (Model)	129
Oysters a la Catalan	83
A la Poulette	17
Omelette	60
Peaches a la Princesse	134
Planked Fillet Mignon	61
Polenti	99
Quajatole en Mole	133
Rice, Spanish	9
Milanaise	51
Italian	132
Riena Cabot	135
Salad, Italian	131
Palace Grill	62
Oyster	130
Sauer Braten	48
Sauce, Delmonico Raisin	33
Caramel	135
Mushroom	131
Scrapple	97
Shrimp Creole, Antoine	84
Snails Bordelaise	53
Soup: Bisque of Crawfish	89
Creole Gumbo	130
Onion	130
Sultana Roll	135
Sweetbreads Scalloped	132
Turta (Italian)	132
Toulous Ragout	132
Tamales	98
Tagliarini des Beaux Arts	117
Terrapin a la Maryland	18
Wines, How to Serve	127
Welsh Rarebit	135
Zabaoine	134
Restaurants	
Blanco's	17, 42
Bonini's Barn	44
Buon Gusto	25
Castilian	44
Coppa's	36
Fashion, Charlie's	44
Felix	17, 43
Fior d'Italia	25
Fly Trap	44
Frank's	43
Fred Solari's	65
Gianduja	50
Hang Far Low	55
Heidelberg Inn	46
Hof Brau	48
Hotel St. Francis	63
Jack's	43
Jule's	25, 44
La Madrelina	44
Leon d'Oro	52
Luna's	31
Mint	15, 43
Negro's	43
Odeon	44
Palace Hotel	19, 60
Poodle Dog	17, 42
Poodle Dog—Bergez-Frank's	16, 43
Portola-Louvre	41
Rathskeller	48
Shell Fish Grotto	80
Solari's	65
Tait's	42
Techau's	42
Vesuvius	81
Old Time Restaurants	

INDEX

Bab's	27	Marchand's		14
Baldwin Hotel	18	Marshall's Chop House		14
Bazzuro's	12, 78	Martin's		15
Bergez	17	Maison Doree		17
California House	13	Nevada		13
Call	16	New York		17
Captain Cropper	18	Old Louvre		27
Campi's	25	Perini's		14
Christian Good	14	Pierre		16
Cliff House	21	Poodle Dog		16
Cobweb Palace	19	Pup		16
Delmonico	16	Peter Job		17
El Dorado House	10	Palace of Art		20
Frank's	17	Pop Floyd		25
Gobey's	87	Reception		18
Good Fellows' Grotto	26	Sanguinetti's		23
Hoffman House	26	Tehama House		13
Iron House	10	Three Trees		17
Johnson's Oyster House	14	Tortoni		16
Jack's	17	Thompson's		27, 41
Louvre	26	Viticultural		25
Ma Tanta	12	Zinkand's		27
Manning's	13			

HERE END BOHEMIAN SAN FRANCISCO—
ITS RESTAURANTS AND THEIR MOST FA-
MOUS RECIPES, AS WRITTEN BY CLARENCE
E. EDWORDS. PUBLISHED IN BOOK FORM
BY PAUL ELDER & COMPANY, AND SEEN
THROUGH THEIR TOMOYE PRESS BY JOHN
SWART IN THE CITY OF SAN FRANCISCO,
DURING THE MONTH OF NOVEMBER, NINE-
TEEN HUNDRED AND FOURTEEN.

Made in the USA
Las Vegas, NV
21 July 2022